SEARCH

We had positioned ourselves to impact downtown Jackson, we just needed a leader. The success came when the pastor search committee partnered with Vanderbloemen. It worked better than we ever dreamed it would.

—**Bob Gladney**, Executive Pastor, First Baptist Jackson

Due to finances, we had limited resources to operate a lengthy Senior Pastor search on our own. This hire could make or break the church's future, and we didn't want to risk it with our little hiring experience. God truly used Vanderbloemen to assemble an amazing staff. Three of our four full-time staff were found through Vanderbloemen.

—**Andy Hahn**, Executive Pastor,
Far Hills Community Church

William Vanderbloemen has successfully assisted countless churches in the search for the best leaders for their congregations. I commend *Search* to any church, in any denomination, that aspires to lead a thorough, efficient process for transition.

—**Thom Rainer**, president of LifeWay Christian Resources,
best-selling author of *I Am a Church Member*

Christ Church had never been through a Senior Pastor search process, and after thirty-one years of ministry under a founding rector, we needed their help. William and his team entered the Anglican tribe with courage and confidence armed only with a list of contacts. They learned our polity and found us a candidate who is pitch perfect for our position. Mission accomplished!

—**Rev. David Roseberry**, Rector, Christ Church

SEARCH

THE PASTORAL SEARCH COMMITTEE HANDBOOK

WILLIAM VANDERBLOEMEN

PUBLISHING GROUP

NASHVILLE, TENNESSEE

978-1-4336-8989-5

Published by B&H Publishing Group
Nashville, Tennessee

Dewey Decimal Classification: 253
Subject Heading: PASTOR SEARCH COMMITTEE \
CLERGY \ MINISTERS

3 4 5 6 7 8 9 • 24 23 22 21 20

CONTENTS

Chapter 1   You Need an Organ Transplant   1

Chapter 2   Where to Start—the Biblical Foundation
              for Search   5

Chapter 3   So You Need a New Pastor?   17

Chapter 4   Forming the Pastor Search Committee   31

Chapter 5   The Pastor Search Process   51

Chapter 6   Know Your Church   69

Chapter 7   Know Who's Out There   87

Chapter 8   Figure Out Who's a Match   95

Chapter 9   Landing the Plane—the Hiring Process   109

Chapter 10 Conclusion   129

Appendices

  A.   Pastor Search Committee Prayer Calendar   133

  B.   Sample Pastor Search Committee Member
       Agreement   139

C. Sample Pastor Search Committee Retreat
    Agenda   143

D. Sample Pastor Search Committee Meeting
    Agenda   145

E. Reference Check Authorization Form   147

F. Sample Reference Check Format   151

G. Listening Guide for Evaluating
    Teaching/Sermon Samples   153

H. List of Personality Assessments   159

I. Sample Senior Pastor Profile/Job Description   163

J. Sample Church Profile   165

K. Sample On-Site Interview Format   167

L. Sample Senior Pastor Interview Questions   171

M. Sample Succession/Senior Pastor Search
    Time Line   173

About the Author   177

About Vanderbloemen Search Group   179

Acknowledgments   183

Chapter 1

YOU NEED AN ORGAN TRANSPLANT

If you're reading this book, then it is likely you have a role in helping your church find its next pastor. Thanks for letting me into this sacred space in your church's life. I know that the process can be daunting and filled with anxiety. And if you're on a search committee for your next pastor, chances are you've never hired a pastor before. That can make an already weighty task even more anxious. Having been a part of over seven hundred pastoral searches, I promise you there is light at the end of the tunnel. And hopefully this book can serve as a roadmap toward that light.

Finding your church's pastor is as serious as an organ transplant. Bringing an outsider into your body to run a major system is a critical process that warrants expert help.

You need a pastor who matches your church's vision, work ethic, culture, and most importantly, your church's heart.

Every church faces leadership changes. Leadership transitions often negatively affect the life of the church. Ministries are halted, church members leave, and giving slows down. The momentum the church was building is lost.

Imagine instead if the church had a process already in place. What if they knew how to form a search committee and begin the search process for the person God was calling to lead their church? There is no magic formula for planning a seamless pastor search, but I've written this handbook to help make the process easier for churches by providing pastor search committees, church leaders, and pastors a guide to planning for the overwhelming pastor search process.

> You need a pastor who matches your church's vision, work ethic, culture, and most importantly, your church's heart.

The average church takes twelve to twenty-four months to find a new pastor when the previous pastor vacates the pulpit. This is a huge challenge to the church, as momentum and direction is lost and members leave. What if, instead of wasting time on direction-less meetings and losing momentum from pulpitless Sundays, pastor search committees knew exactly which steps to take to lead their congregation toward discerning the Lord's next leader for their church?

Search will help your church successfully navigate each stage in finding your next pastor by providing clear steps for forming, guiding, and successfully executing the pastoral search process.

In this handbook, you will learn how to:

- minimize the painful loss of momentum your church will experience without a pastor;
- recognize the specific stage of pastoral succession the church is in (i.e., emergency succession, pastoral retirement, etc.);
- form a customized time line and communication plan for your unique search situation;
- possess the tools necessary for creating an effective job description, compensation package, interviewing guidelines, and communication plan; and
- identify the anxiety often experienced by churches in the pastor search process and how to address it in your congregation.

You'll also learn from our experience. Over the years, we have worked with several hundred churches and tens of thousands of candidates. We have included many stories from real-life searches we have helped conduct. For confidentiality's sake, we have refrained from using the churches' names. But we would urge you to pay close attention to these examples and learn from them.

I've often said that the expert isn't necessarily smarter than everyone else but is the one who has more experience. Learn from our repetitions. We have seen search done well, and we have learned what not to do along the way. Our hope is that we can keep you from making mistakes we have seen over the years and that this book will guide you and your church toward a smooth and successful search.

Put on your seat belt and let's dive into the pastor search committee process together.

Chapter 2

WHERE TO START—THE BIBLICAL FOUNDATION FOR SEARCH

In the hustle and bustle of forming your committee, it can be easy to forget that we are only a tool in God's process of bringing a new pastor to His church. Over the years of doing searches with churches, I've become convinced that the key asset we bring to God's process is prayer. Prayer moves the hands that move the world, and it's the single most important part of your search.

While the process is important, don't forget that the purpose of the process is to seek the one whom God is already raising up to be your pastor.

A small church of one hundred in rural North Carolina had been searching for a pastor for more than a year when they called me. This church was rich in history, originating in 1748. They had a wonderful interim pastor who was leading them while they started their search for a Senior Pastor. With limited financial resources, they felt hopeless. According to Tim, their interim pastor, "The church was one generation away from extinction."

I hear stories like this from churches on a daily basis. Our humanness often draws us to focus on minutiae in an attempt to exercise some kind of control over a situation filled with unknowns. When you keep the Holy Spirit as a guide throughout the process, you'll be able to see God's hand through each step.

As we guided the church through a search process led by prayer, the committee was able to find their Senior Pastor four months later. It is vital that the search committee keeps Christ at the center of the search process and not be distracted by agenda or rigidness of polity.

Here are a few ways that you can keep your search committee focused on discerning whom God is calling to fill the vacant role on your church staff:

Pray Expectantly

The importance of prayer during this process is difficult to overstate. Pray both individually and as a search committee regularly and expectantly. We see the power of prayer on a daily basis as we help our clients discern whom God is calling to serve at their church.

Open each of your pastor search committee meetings with prayer. Here are a couple of verses to guide your prayers.

"Ask and it will be given to you; seek and you will find; knock and the door will be opened to you. For everyone who asks receives; the one who seeks finds; and to the one who knocks, the door will be opened." (Matt. 7:7–8)

Pray Intentionally

Jesus used an intentional order in the Lord's Prayer in Matthew 6, where His primary focus is God and His glory. Set up an intentional prayer schedule for your pastor search committee using this model. Some points of intention for prayer (for which we will later provide scriptural resources) can be:

- Discernment
- Guidance
- Unity
- Cohesion
- Patience
- Church staff
- Pastor search committee
- Outgoing pastor and family
- Incoming pastor and family

When you ask, you do not receive, because you ask with wrong motives. . . . (James 4:3)

Keep a Humble Heart

One of the biggest stumbling blocks we see pastor search committees face is members of the committee who are naysayers or place their personal agenda above what is best for the church. These members of the search committee are toxic to the search process and can make it very difficult for the entire committee to discern whom God is calling to the church. Remember these verses in Philippians and Mark to avoid being one of the negative search committee members:

> Do nothing out of selfish ambition or vain conceit. Rather, in humility value others above yourselves, not looking to your own interests but each of you to the interests of the others. (Phil. 2:3–4)

> And they came to Capernaum. And when he was in the house he asked them, "What were you discussing on the way?" But they kept silent, for on the way they had argued with one another about who was the greatest. And he sat down and called the twelve. And he said to them, "If anyone would be first, he must be last of all and servant of all." (Mark 9:33–35 ESV)

Fellowship Together

A successful search committee comes down to people, and building trust among your committee members is crucial to a successful search. Jesus, who knew our hearts perfectly, often encouraged intentional social interaction. Spend quality time together as a team where you don't talk about the search and solely focus on getting to know each other better. Have meals together. Ask each other about how you came to know Christ, your family, work life, and hobbies. When you understand each other well, you'll have less conflict and be able to focus on Christ during your search process.

> How good and pleasant it is when God's people live together in unity! (Ps. 133:1)

Fast Together

There is great power in fasting. When we exercise control over what we put into our bodies, we are engaging in an exercise of obedience. What the body does, often the heart will follow. When we have a restless heart, fasting can draw us nearer to the Lord. Fasting corporately can foster great feelings of unity. For these reasons, seek the Lord through fasting as a committee and a congregation.

There are many forms of fasting. Fasting can mean abstaining from one meal a week or for a whole day, spending that time in prayer. But fasting can also mean restricting your diet to certain foods as Daniel did in Daniel 10:2, now called the "Daniel Fast," in order to understand better the revelation that was given him.

"Do not be afraid, Daniel. Since the first day that
you set your mind to gain understanding and to
humble yourself before your God, your words were
heard, and I have come in response to them." (Dan.
10:12)

Remember Christ's Promises

Be intentional about the Scripture you personally and the
team collectively is ingesting during your pastoral search process. Curate a collection of Scriptures to read together before
meetings, before prayer, before meals. Focus on Scripture passages where God highlights His vast goodness and greatness.

As the heavens are higher than the earth, so are my
ways higher than your ways and my thoughts than
your thoughts. (Isa. 55:9)

Behold, You have made the heavens and the earth
by Your great power and by Your outstretched arm!
Nothing is too difficult for You. (Jer. 32:17 NASB)

Now to Him who is able to do far more abundantly
beyond all that we ask or think, according to the
power that works within us. (Eph. 3:20 NASB)

"I am the good shepherd; the good shepherd lays
down His life for the sheep." (John 10:11 NASB)

Jesus is our good shepherd, and He promises to lead us if we are His. We can trust that He's leading every step of the pastoral search process.

Throughout the search process, it is helpful to pray for specific themes that the search committee and involved parties will face during the time line. Following are some pieces of Scripture and overarching themes of prayer that are helpful in each particular stage in the process.

Guidance

At the beginning of the search, the pastoral search committee should create a time line and a pastoral profile for your church's ideal candidates based on the church's ministry needs, vision, mission, and values.

Pray that the true needs of the congregation will come to the surface as the church staff and committee seek the Lord about what is next for your church. Pray that no personal agenda would surface but only the will of the Lord as the search committee and staff seek what He has next for the congregation.

> And God placed all things under his feet and appointed him to be head over everything for the church, which is his body, the fullness of him who fills everything in every way. (Eph. 1:22–23)

And it is my prayer that your love may abound
more and more, with knowledge and all discernment, so that you may approve what is excellent,
and so be pure and blameless for the day of Christ,
filled with the fruit of righteousness that comes
through Jesus Christ, to the glory and praise of God.
(Phil. 1:9–11 ESV)

Unity

As the pastor search committee writes the job description
for the pastor profile based on the needs of your church, pray
for unity. This process has the potential to divide the committee on details of the description and the profile. It is of the
utmost importance that your pastor search committee stay
unified and focused on the spirit of the search.

Pray that the pastor search committee will have clarity as
to the characteristics, goals, and key result areas that should
be included in the job description for the church's next pastor.
Pray that the committee would not settle for too little or aim
too high, making the job description unreasonable or unattainable. Pray that the committee would agree upon the background and experience needed in the next pastor.

The saying is trustworthy: If anyone aspires to
the office of overseer, he desires a noble task.
Therefore an overseer must be above reproach.
(1 Tim. 3:1–2 ESV)

I appeal to you, brothers, by the name of our
Lord Jesus Christ, that all of you agree, and that
there be no divisions among you, but that you be
united in the same mind and the same judgment.
(1 Cor. 1:10 ESV)

Discernment

There are great systems and processes in this book for your
pastoral search, but choosing the right pastor is much more of
an art than a science. You can set up testing and systems, check
references, and listen to sermons, but at the end of the day, you
as a committee will have to make a judgment call. Search is a
spiritual exercise in discernment.

The verse I reflect upon as I pray every morning is Luke
2:52, "Jesus grew in wisdom, and stature, and in favor with God
and man." If Jesus was born 100 percent perfect, and He grew
in wisdom, then that's growth I probably need too. I've found
that if you'll ask God for wisdom, He will not turn you down.
He considered it Solomon's best possible request for a prayer.
Praying for discernment daily might be the single best task you
as a committee can do.

Your pastor search committee will begin receiving and
evaluating applications from candidates. During this time, it
is easy to stray from the time line your pastor search committee established during the previous months. It is important to
stay focused and hungry for God's Word rather than indulge
distractions.

Pray that the committee will hear God's voice with clarity and feel peace as they discern whom they should interview. Pray that as they read applications, listen to sermon samples, and talk with candidates, they place the church's needs and desires before their own.

> "I am the good shepherd; I know my sheep and my sheep know me." (John 10:14)

Patience

Toward the middle and end of the search process, the pastor search committee will begin interviewing candidates with the most promise to be the church's next pastor. During this time, it's common for your pastor search committee to be eager. While being eager is not a bad or even misplaced emotion, it can lead to rushed decisions. Some search committees love every candidate while others can't see any candidate as being able to fill the role. Approach the interviews with a patient and open heart, and God will see to it that they bear much fruit.

Pray that the pastor search committee will know the right questions to ask as they represent the church through the interview process. Pray that they will represent the church accurately and attractively. Pray for patience as your pastor search committee considers each candidate, providing equal time and attention to each one. Pray that they will have clarity as they interview candidates, eliminate candidates, and move forward with candidates throughout the interview process.

In the same way, let your light shine before others,
so that they may see your good works and give glory
to your Father who is in heaven. (Matt. 5:16 ESV)

Wisdom

The pastor search committee will begin narrowing the
pool of candidates down to a few finalists and begin praying
over whom God has called to lead the church. This might mean
that the committee has a finalist who is currently in view of a
call. As the pastor search committee continues to talk through
each finalist, it is important to rest in God's wisdom instead of
debating with an anxious heart.

Pray that the future pastor, spouse, and family would feel
the same peace and excitement that the pastor search committee feels about the candidate. Pray that the candidate and his
family will have clarity during their visits with the church and
know whether or not this is the next step in ministry to which
God has called them.

And the peace of God, which passeth all understanding, shall keep your hearts and minds through
Christ Jesus. (Phil. 4:7 KJV)

Transition

Toward the end of the search, the pastor search committee
will likely submit an offer to the church's next pastor.

Pray that the entire congregation would feel a sense of peace and confirmation as the pastor is confirmed through congregational meetings and/or a congregational voting process. Pray there is unity among the search committee, church staff, and congregation. Pray that no one person would have an agenda that would cause a distraction or deterrent from God's work throughout the pastor search process. Pray that the new pastor and his family have a smooth transition into their new church and community.

> Above all, clothe yourselves with love, which ties
> everything together in unity. (Col. 3:14 isv)

As the pastor search committee focuses on Christ and seeks His direction, they will receive clarity and peace as they seek whom God is calling next to the church.

Pastoral transitions are trying times, but trying times are the times when believers end up doing some of their best praying. So when you feel nervous, like the weight of a huge decision is on you, or ill equipped for the job of a search, you have an opportunity to pray and see God move in powerful ways.

Chapter 3

SO YOU NEED A NEW PASTOR?

There are generally three causes for the loss of a Senior Pastor: Emergency and Unforeseen Departure, Retirement, or an Unsurprising and Unforeseen Departure. Each of these effects the church and community in different ways. These effects are not only emotional but are often seen in practical daily pieces of the church's rhythm.

> Before the pastor search committee begins the search process, they should identify the type of loss they are experiencing and set expectations for moving forward.

Before the pastor search committee begins the search process, they should identify the type of loss they are experiencing and set expectations for moving forward.

Having walked alongside many churches in a pastoral transition over the years, we've seen the good, the bad, and the ugly. The insights gained from being in the trenches with them are invaluable and worth sharing to help you begin a healthy pastor search process.

These are the three main types of transitions, along with the emotions and challenges attached to each. Each of the following pastoral departures are explained in detail in my book *Next: Pastoral Succession That Works*. Below you will find a brief overview of how each one affects the congregation and pastoral search process.

Emergency and Unforeseen Departure

An emergency and unforeseen departure can be the most difficult and taxing on a congregation. The most common emergency departures are due to moral failure, sickness, and unexpected death.

All of these are painful, heavy, and extremely sensitive circumstances to navigate. Though all of these are messy and unpredictable, many churches stand stronger on the other side of them with God's grace and an intentional healing process.

Moral Failure

It is next to impossible to be prepared for the hurt and shock you feel when a church leader disappoints you. The confusion and betrayal initially felt is often quickly followed by the fear and anxiety of replacing that person. Pastor search committees often feel paralyzed with fear when beginning the search process following a moral failure because they don't want it to happen again. What can you do to rebuild trust during the pastor search process?

1. TRUST IN GOD, NOT MAN

Psalm 18 reminds us that it is better to take refuge in the Lord than to trust in humans. Actively trusting in God may seem action-less, but it is not impact-less. Your church will be looking to your pastor search committee for hope. The peace that comes from focusing on God's faithfulness is powerful, contagious, and a testimony to the truth that faith is the certainty of the things unseen.

2. SEEK CLOSURE REGARDING THE OUTGOING PASTOR

Spend time as a church and search committee seeking closure. That may include bringing in an outside expert or counselor or identifying specific parts of the ministry that may need extra care.

Most importantly, ensure your leadership team is supporting the healing of the outgoing pastor. Many churches will pay for the outgoing pastor's counseling process as well as his family's counseling. It may be helpful to provide a generous severance package to the outgoing pastor to care for the pastor and his family during the transition.

Loving someone who has hurt you is easier said than done, but remember that your church's reaction to your pastor's failure can be a powerful demonstration of God's love and faithfulness.

3. REEVALUATE POLICIES AND PROCEDURES

Are there any changes your church can make to safeguard from the situation happening again? What are some blind spots that might have led to the moral failure? Are there processes in place to maintain the emotional and spiritual health of your church staff? Are there policies to establish accountability? Make an emotional/spiritual health check part of your staff review process if it is not already.

Be cautious that your self-reflection doesn't turn into a blame game. The goal is to restore the church, not to divide or place blame. Keep focused on the vision and mission of your church through every step of the process.

4. Don't hire out of fear

Too often I've seen searches following a moral failure lead a church to call a pastor who is the direct antithesis of their outgoing pastor. It's a natural inclination that sounds something like, "Well we don't want to go through that again, so let's hire someone completely different." Sometimes that's the right idea. Sometimes it's not. The key to knowing the difference between the two is knowing whether or not you are hiring out of fear or out of prayerful discernment.

Sickness and Death

Losing a pastor suddenly to sickness or death is traumatizing as well. As one can imagine, this is extremely heavy and sensitive territory. Grief is a messy, intrusive, unpredictable, and impolite emotion. There are no "best practices" and no magic twelve-step program when grieving the loss of a pastor. Church staffs and congregations will mourn in many different ways.

Our team has walked alongside many churches in this situation over the years, and here are a few things they've done to heal well.

1. Grieve, then celebrate

Grieving will seem like a natural by-product of this loss, but there has to be time given to allow it to happen. There's no fixing this type of situation or sweeping it aside. Give your congregation, your staff, and the family time to grieve.

Then, you must celebrate. Your church not only must celebrate your pastor's life and contribution, you must celebrate the fact that this world is not our home.

2. Give space for questions

When tragedy happens, questions follow: "Why would this happen? How could God allow this to be? What could we have done to help or stop it?"

There must be space for these questions and time allowed to ask them. We've seen plenty of times when this wasn't permitted, and the fall out from the congregation was tragic. Trust in the leadership is lost, and comfort is sought elsewhere.

3. Love your staff

Carve out intentional and specific ways to love the church staff. A church team often functions more like a family, so the loss of a leader is felt much heavier than losing a coworker.

Here are a few ideas on how to provide comfort and support to your church staff during this time:

- Offer opportunities for counseling and small group discussions.
- Allow for some extra paid time off.
- Organize a private memorial for the staff only to share and pray with one another.

Intentionally recognizing the hurt and grieving of the staff will allow the room needed for healing.

4. DON'T CONFUSE HIRING A NEW PASTOR WITH FORGETTING YOUR DECEASED PASTOR

We've worked with many churches in this scenario, and many times the search committee gets held up on hiring a new pastor because they feel they owe it to the previous pastor to wait a while before hiring. Clearly, you don't want to hire too soon, but most churches make the mistake of waiting too long. There is no prescribed grieving period for a lost loved one, and the same is true of a pastor.

Retirement

Bittersweet is the most common word used when a Senior Pastor retires. No matter if he was the founding pastor or only with the church for five years, it is still a difficult transition for the church. Ideally, the congregation has had some time to prepare for and process this transition, thus making it smoother. However, it is still necessary to take extra steps to ensure the best transition possible.

1. Communicate the Plan

This means communication of all aspects of this transition. When is the pastor stepping down? How can the church show him and his family love during this time? Will he still be involved with the church or taking some time away? What is the plan for the pastoral search?

Keeping the church community informed of what is happening and when it is happening goes a long way toward keeping everyone engaged and moving forward.

2. Celebrate the Past, Champion the Future

Celebrating the legacy and ministry of an outgoing Senior Pastor is a natural part of the transition and one that should not be overlooked. A word of caution to the search committee is to avoid aggrandizement of the outgoing pastor. This can cast a dark shadow over the search for your successor and set unrealistic expectations.

After time is given to celebrate the outgoing Senior Pastor's legacy and ministry, the church and search committee must change their language to the future tense. Reiterate the church's vision and plan for the future and the trajectory of the ministries. Promote the excitement and promise of this future leader. Cast a vision for how the church body will come together to keep moving forward into its next chapter.

3. Be Sure the Outgoing Pastor Is Set and Stable to Move Forward

One of the most overlooked details of a retiring Senior Pastor is, "What's next?" Do they have another ministry ahead of them to pour into? Are they financially stable? Will they continue to worship with this community, or are there plans to move on?

All of these details are important not only for the outgoing pastor but also for the church and the possible future candidates. This is a start to a new season for the church, so having the former pastor settled will ensure a much smoother transition for the new pastor.

Unforeseen/Unsurprising

This category encompasses many different reasons for a pastoral transition: a call to the mission field, conflict among leadership, stagnant growth, or a call to another church. Though there are different causes, they generally fall into two different categories: departure among conflict or departure during peacetime.

Departure among Conflict

This is unfortunate but not uncommon for churches of all sizes to experience. A pastor is asked to step down for financial reasons, there's conflict among leadership or about the vision of the church, or maybe the church's growth is stagnate. These are all common when a pastor steps down out of conflict.

1. BE DIRECT IN COMMUNICATION TO THE CHURCH

Churches are often tempted to try to protect the congregation from too much information. In doing so, they usually create more questions, more controversy, and more division. It is best to be direct and honest. Your church members will feel respected and in turn will give more trust when they know you are being transparent. Tell them what happened, what is being done about it, and how leadership is handling it moving forward. It might not be necessary to share every detail, but you should share as much as necessary to provide direction and clarity about the situation and what is being done to deal with it in a healthy, God-honoring, and redemptive way.

2. BE REDEMPTIVE

One of the many things Jesus teaches us is that even the worst scenarios have the power to be redemptive. A crisis in your church, if handled wisely, can be used by God to create new opportunities for growth and new vitality in your community. The goal in this transition is to keep the door open for God to bring His redemptive and healing power to your church and your community.

Departure during Peacetime

This type of transition is for many different reasons, but the departure is peaceful and often leaves feelings of fondness among the church community for the outgoing pastor.

To foster an environment where the pastor can leave in peaceful conditions, consider the following.

1. HAVE A PROCESS FOR SUCCESSION

Chapter 2 from my book *Next: Pastoral Succession That Works* discusses the ten commandments of succession planning. Have your church leadership implement these ten steps well before a pastoral search is needed to set up your church for long-term health. Then, when the pastorate is vacated, church leadership will know exactly what to do next.

2. Create a Leadership Culture of Rest and Open Conversation

The Senior Pastor should have senior leaders around him with whom he can confidentially discuss his long-term thoughts and plans for his vocation. The pastorate can be a lonely and tiresome place, and tired pastors make mistakes. Create a culture that values sabbaticals and rest so that pastors can keep a healthy pace. Additionally, create a leadership culture at your church where the pastors have leaders around them who welcome honest conversation about how they are feeling and where they need support. Then there are support systems in place to help decrease the chance of a pastor fleeing from conflict.

Communication

Clear and consistent communication of your pastoral transition is paramount to the success of your search. It not only keeps the congregation involved and engaged, but it also garners support for the search committee efforts and sets proper expectations for the process and timing of the search.

One of the first things the committee should do before launching the search process is establish a communication strategy. The communication strategy will look different for each church's unique transition. However, there are helpful steps that every church should take in making sure their pastoral transition is properly communicated to its church community.

1. Create a Dedicated Landing Page on Your Website

Ideally, your church should ideally already have an employment section on your website where you post job opportunities and information on how potential candidates can apply to work with your church. This gives you a chance to describe the church's staff culture, a brief yet thorough description of each of the open positions, and specific action steps for candidates who are interested in applying.

When communicating to your church about a Senior Pastor transition, create an additional landing page dedicated to updating your community about the search process. Once your church leadership team has decided to move forward with the pastor search, the first thing you should do is set up a meeting with your web team about developing a dedicated landing page for the search. If you don't have a web team, consider asking a member of your church community who is experienced in simple web development or blogging to help you set up a platform to keep your church updated online about the pastor search process.

A few tips regarding the pastor search landing page on your church's website:

- Make the landing page easy to find on the front page of your website, as congregational members will want to check in periodically about the process.
- Include bios and information about the search committee.
- Describe the process you are going through with an anticipated time line.

- If applicable, include information about any outside help you are using such as a search firm or consulting group.
- List the preferred contact information so that interested candidates can easily contact the search committee.

Your members want to be informed on the search process. Having an updated landing page with answers to frequently asked questions will help alleviate the influx of questions your church staff and pastor search committee may receive upon the announcement of the pastor search.

2. Record and Post a Video of the Outgoing Pastor's Announcement

Posting a video announcement is a helpful way to help your church community process the transition that is taking place. Not every Senior Pastor transition will have the ability to make this a part of their communication plan, but it is extremely useful when possible.

Pastoral transitions are difficult for church members, and allowing them to hear the announcement directly from the pastor will lessen the confusion and hearsay that can often follow a pastor's transition announcement. It also mitigates the chances of people hearing different versions of "what happened." Finally, it allows everyone to hear at the same time. If you're in a church with more than one worship service (or more than one campus), serious consideration should be given to a video announcement. In the case of retirement, your outgoing pastor can also write about his succession plan on his personal blog, which is one of the most effective ways pastors can communicate with your church community about his own transition process.

3. Be Consistent

Once you have your landing page set up, ensure that it is updated consistently. It is frustrating to church members when they are trying to find information about the pastor search process and see an outdated page. Be sure it is one person's responsibility, either on the pastor search committee or church staff, to keep the website updated as the search progresses.

4. Have a Communication Plan

It is vital to the long-term health of your church that both your church staff and your church community know whom to contact for information regarding the pastor search process. Make sure that everyone knows where the job description can be found online, the e-mail address where candidates' resumes can be sent, and whom to contact for questions and concerns regarding the search. Include this information on your pastor search landing page so that inquirers have clear direction on where to find answers. The last thing you want is for several people to be running point and mixed answers to be given, which will cause confusion for all parties involved.

No matter the way in which your pastor left, your church needs loving guidance to walk alongside them throughout the search process. Change is always hard, regardless of whether it is good or bad. Your search committee has the opportunity to lead your church through this transition and help it become a positive and exciting new season for your congregation.

Chapter 4

FORMING THE PASTOR SEARCH COMMITTEE

When a church has a need to find a new pastor, one of the first steps at many churches is to form a pastor search committee. This committee is especially critical to the church's body because of the sacredness of the pulpit. When a church is searching for a new pastor, it is at a holy crossroads. The church body is often full of anxiety, fear, and conflict as the committee strives to lead the church into a new chapter.

There is no magic formula for the proper structure of a search committee. A church's polity and bylaws play an important role in the formation of the search committee. As examples, here are three churches we have worked with during their search process:

A large Southern Baptist church in Mississippi had many decision makers as a part of their search process. They had a couple hundred deacons, several elders, a personnel committee, and a pastor search committee all involved in their search process.

A nondenominational church in California only had four elders who were solely responsible for finding their Senior Pastor.

A Congregational church in New England had about nine hundred members, and the search process involved almost seven hundred of them at differing levels through town halls and surveys. The search committee for that church had a very different size and function than either of the other two.

We'll discuss best practices and recommendations for forming your search committee in this chapter, but the most important component of a pastor search committee is clarity—clarity of responsibility, decision making, and time line.

Determine How Your Church Makes Decisions

Before you move forward with forming your pastor search committee for your Senior Pastor search, you must have a solid understanding of your church's polity—how the church is organized, who the decision makers are, and the processes for how the church's decision makers make decisions.

Most churches have denominationally guided or self-imposed bylaws and/or established processes for how they make decisions in various scenarios. It is vital that you understand these thoroughly and comply with them throughout the pastor search process. If your church does not have clear bylaws or processes already in place for how decisions are made, then it is necessary for the church leadership to determine those before appointing your pastor search committee.

Here are some questions to help you solidify your church's decision making:

- Does your denomination have bylaws or guidelines you can use as your compass?
- Are the decision makers and the church leadership (the elders, church staff, etc.) in sync with the search committee?
- What is your church's polity, and who needs to be considered a decision maker?

Episcopal Polity

This is a hierarchical church polity where churches are governed by archbishops, bishops, and priests, as seen in Catholic, Orthodox, Anglican, and Episcopal churches. Because these churches have very established processes for making decisions and appointing priests, they do not usually participate in a pastor search process, but rather church leaders are appointed by the higher ranks.

Presbyterian Polity

Elders are the church leaders and decision makers in churches with this type of polity; thus, this leadership structure is also known as elder-led. Presbyterian churches, Reformed churches, Christian churches, and some nondenominational churches use this model of church governance. The session, or group of elders, would most likely make the final decision for a Senior Pastor hire. If your church is elder-led, it is important to determine how the elders and the pastor search committee will work together on the process/decision. Will the committee recommend their top candidates to the elders and the elders make the final decision? Sometimes at elder-led churches, the elders are the pastor search committee.

Congregational Polity

In this type of church polity, the congregation governs itself and creates its own bylaws, as seen in Baptist churches and many nondenominational churches. Decision making can vary within this polity since the churches can determine their own rules. If you are within this polity, who are the decision makers for your church? How is it structured? Is it staff-led, where the church leadership makes the final decisions? Does the Senior Pastor make the final decisions? Is it board-led? Elder-led? Does the congregation through a congregational vote make the decisions? Will the pastor search committee recommend their top candidate to the board or to the congregation for a vote? Who will make the final hire?

No matter the written polity of your church, there is the unwritten reality of how things really get done. Does your search process allow the real decision makers the ability to be involved and/or have buy-in to the process?

Determine the Purpose and Mission of the Pastor Search Committee

Just as a church or organization will flounder without a vision and/or mission statement, so too your pastor search committee needs a vision and mission statement. With no organization or purpose and only the vague idea of "we need to find a pastor," your committee will lack direction and organization.

Begin with your church's mission statement and vision (for more on this, read Chapter 6: Know Your Church) and form your pastor search committee's mission statement from that. If your church doesn't have a clear, succinct mission statement and vision, now is the time to formulate those.

A mission statement is one sentence that describes why your church exists and what it does—what your church is passionate about and how it lives out that passion. A vision statement is one sentence that expresses the long-term goal of your church—the changes you desire to see as a result of the work your church does.

Let's say, for example, your church's mission statement is, to borrow an example from our friends at Community Christian Church in Naperville, Illinois, "Helping people find their way back to God." You could then craft your pastor search committee mission statement to be, "The mission of [church's] pastor search committee is to strategically find and prayerfully hire a discipleship-minded Senior Pastor who will help [church] continue to live out its mission of helping people find their way back to God."

Likewise, you could work backward from your church's vision statement. If your vision statement is something like, "To reach the greater Orlando community for Christ and expand the kingdom of God," then your pastor search committee's mission statement could be, "The mission of [church's] pastor search committee is to seek, discern, and hire the person whom we believe to be the next Lead Pastor of [church]—a servant-leader with a local-missions focus who will lead [church] in its vision to reach the greater Orlando community for Christ and expand the kingdom of God."

By using your church's mission and/or vision statement to form the mission statement of your pastor search committee, you are beginning the pastor search process with a clear direction and end goal. It will also ensure that you are seeking candidates whose gifts and passions align with the goals of your church body.

How Large Should Your Pastor Search Committee Be?

Before you decide who should be on the search committee, you need to determine how large your search committee should be. The suggested size range for a pastor search committee is seven to eleven people. Make sure the committee is an odd number of people, to prevent any stalemates when taking any votes.

> The suggested size range for a pastor search committee is seven to eleven people.

Beware of forming a pastor search committee larger than eleven members. It's important that the committee is able to be nimble. It's difficult to reach any consensus when there are too many opinions involved. The phrase "too many cooks in the kitchen" rings true for pastor search committees too. The more differing opinions and voices that need to be heard on your search committee, the longer the pastor search process will take.

Who Should Be on Your Pastor Search Committee?

There is an old joke that says, "If three Americans, just by chance, bumped into each other on a street corner in Paris—they would form a committee." Americans have had a long love of committees—from government, to schools, to civic clubs. This affinity for committees has become normal operating procedure for the governance of most local churches in our land.

When I was a young pastor, I thought the number one quality to look for when recruiting or appointing church lay leaders was competency. I looked high and low for the biggest leaders, the CEOs of the largest companies, and people with the most letters after their name. I was wrong.

While those qualities are significant, it doesn't necessarily mean those people will make the best elders, deacons, board members, or pastor search committee members. Who will serve on your committee is quite possibly the most important aspect of forming a pastor search committee, as whom you put on the committee will affect what candidates are found and hired, which will in turn shape the direction and future of your church.

Select People Who Are Agenda-Free and Have the Best Interests of the Church at Heart

The conventional wisdom of choosing the members to serve on your pastor search committee is to get people who represent the entire body of the church—every demographic, gender, ministry age group, etc. This may be the conventional wisdom, and you may be trying to include everyone who you believe needs to have a voice in the decision; but we've seen that this approach often doesn't work. When a church takes this approach, then each of the members may strive to be the voice of their specific demographic and its agenda, resulting in many different ideas of what to look for in their next pastor—even with the best of intentions.

Instead of trying to represent every group of the church (who might each be mostly concerned with their age group, ministry, or demographic in the church's future), find people for your pastor search committee who have in mind the best interests of the church as a whole and who have broad enough perspective to see beyond their own personal preferences and needs. Select people who have spiritual depth, who have a broad vision for the church and its mission, and who truly want what's best for the church and not what's best for them.

Though you don't need to represent every single ministry or demographic, it is important to have a mix of generations. Most importantly, have a committee representative of the people your church is trying to reach. For example, if one of the main missions of your church is to reach the next generation for Christ and you're searching for a pastor who is talented at speaking to the younger generation, don't have a pastor search committee made up of only people over fifty. Just as your pastor search committee mission statement should align with the church's mission/vision statement, so should the members of the pastor search committee align with those who understand and are part of the vision and mission of your church.

Some churches have one (or a few) "squeaky wheels," the somewhat difficult person who insists on having a say, giving their critique of things, and being heard. It may be tempting to put this type of person on the pastor search committee thinking, "If we give them a voice in the decision, they won't complain about it after the person they chose is here." While this may seem logical at first, it's a quick way to torpedo your pastor search process. This type of person can bog down the entire process. It's vitally important to choose people who are agenda-free, who can set aside what they personally want in their next pastor and think about the big picture and the good of the whole church.

Select People Who Are Available for and Committed to the Committee and Process

It's vitally important to select people for your search committee who are available and committed. Many pastor search committees have their members sign a member agreement or covenant outlining clearly what they are committing to and giving a written word of their dedication to seeing the pastor search process through (see Appendix B for a sample of such an agreement).

Don't put people on the search committee whose schedules don't allow them to invest significant time in the process. Sometimes pastor search committees are filled or led by gifted people who have demonstrated excellence in their workplace as well as in ministry. These people are great voices to have, but in some cases their work will pull them away from the pastor search process at critical moments. Choose members who are able to make their role on the search committee a priority for this season.

You also don't want people on your search committee who have nothing but time on their hands. You don't want this decision about who to hire for their next pastor to be their life's ambition. They need to be people who have balanced, well-prioritized lives and who have demonstrated a commitment to serving your church.

Select People Who Live Out the Church's Mission and Vision

Every one of the best pastor search committee members has had this one common trait: a passion for the mission of the church. That's not to be confused with a passion for their personal vision for how they would run the church. When looking for a pastor search committee member, think carefully about how they are living out the mission and vision of the church. Can you see it in their life? When you interview them about the possibility of joining the committee, do they refer to the mission and vision of the church?

Select People Who Match the Culture of the Church and Staff

Similar to the point above, great pastor search committees "fit" the culture of the church and ideally fit the staff culture as well. They reflect the type of person who is the bull's-eye for the mission of the church. If your church is targeting people in poverty and recovery, the best board members might be people who don't have a fancy title or job but do have experience in recovery and have lived in (and overcome) poverty.

Additionally, when assessing culture fit (and vision fit), don't forget to measure your potential committee member's character. Does your potential committee member reflect the kind of disciple that you would want representing spiritual maturity for your church?

Select People Who Possess Expertise That Complements the Needs of the Church

What is the focus of your ministry? What are the key strategic needs of the church? If you are a church that is reaching many unchurched people, chances are that your ministry is growing faster than your income/tithing. Find committee members who understand your church's unique challenges in your community and have the expertise to provide solutions to those challenges. This is especially important with a pastor search committee since they will be helping discern whom God is calling to lead the church and cast vision for the church's role in the community. Find people who possess the skills and experience that match the specific needs of your church.

Select People Who Exude a Non-Anxious Presence

Effective pastor search committee members exude a "non-anxious presence" (what we call the ability to take a NAP) and are unflappable. When the water gets choppy, as it does in the church world and during the pastor search process, having a pastor search committee that doesn't flip out or act anxious will be a lifesaver. We've seen some churches that have gone through hell but survived well. And nearly every time, you can draw a straight line back to a pastor search committee made up of levelheaded, Christ-centered people.

Select People Who Are Supportive but Can Think Independently and Can Balance the Two

Loyalty is paramount in effective pastor search committees. Too many churches are set up for an adversarial relationship between committees and the pastor. I've never seen that produce an effective, growing church. Effective pastor search committees see their role as advisors and supporters to the pastor and church staff, but not managers or watchdogs.

By the same token, the most effective pastor search committee members are able to think for themselves. Committee members are not "yes" people who are unable to give an independent opinion. They always put the church's vision before their own when making decisions.

Select People Who Understand the Importance of Planning for Succession

As I say in the preface of *Next: Pastoral Succession That Works*, every pastor is an interim pastor. It's said that there are only two certainties in life: death and taxes. I've come to believe there's a third: pastoral succession. Unless your church closes, or the Lord Jesus returns, it will face at least one, if not many, pastoral transitions. But the conversation about succession is a difficult one to start and a nervous matter for a pastor to bring up. In most churches, pastor search committees are formed after the pastor has already left. How much more effective could your church be if you had a pastor search committee whose function also included planning for your current pastor's succession, no matter his tenure in the pastorate? Having a board or committee that initiates and supports this conversation is a real asset to pastors and can be a "legacy saver" for the church.

In fact, in chapter 2 of *Next: Pastoral Succession That Works*, the "first commandment" of preparing for succession is "Read this book with others." Whether it's emergency planning or long-term planning, good committee members will help initiate a succession conversation in a way that helps and doesn't threaten the pastor.

Select People Who Do Not Micromanage the Church

Elder means "overseer," not "micromanager." Effective pastor search committees know the difference and are able to oversee in a way that liberates the pastor and staff to execute the vision of the church. Effective pastor search committee members do not overstep their bounds of leadership or attempt to control things outside of their influence.

Find pastor search committee members who can balance oversight with trust. The best pastor search committees can provide accountability and oversight for the leadership team throughout the search process but then also rely on and trust the competency of the church staff who have their heads in the game 24/7.

Select People Who Have Leadership Experience

Your church board members should have leadership experience. Seek people who have a track record of hard work and leadership success. If you want your church to grow and develop, then you need to have people on your church board who have experience growing and developing the organizations they have been a part of. The very best board members are comfortable in top leadership positions and know the importance of staying up to date on best practices in business, staffing, management, and use of technology.

Select People Who Play Well with Others

Getting along with others is another key factor to successful candidates in our searches, and it's the same with pastor search committee members. As I mentioned earlier, churches often make the mistake of naming a "naysayer" to the committee. The rationale is that if they include the loudly negative person, then that person will have input into the decisions of the committee and will quit complaining.

I've never seen that work. In fact, I have always seen it backfire in spades. Find people who listen, who are collaborative, and who communicate well—and not in a negative manner—with others.

Also, effective pastor search committee members are loyal to each other. Your committee should be made up of people who can disagree in a meeting or vote against the majority, yet walk out of the meeting fully owning and supporting the decision of the board.

Here is a helpful checklist summing up all of the traits we recommend seeking in pastor search committee members:

- They are agenda-free.
- They have spiritual depth.
- They have a broad view of the church and its mission, and have its best interests at heart.
- They are available for and committed to the committee and process.
- They live out the church's mission and vision.
- They match the culture of the church and staff.
- They possess expertise that complements the needs of the church.
- They exude a non-anxious presence.
- They understand the importance of planning for succession.
- They are supportive but can think independently . . . and can balance the two.
- They do not micromanage the church.
- They have leadership experience.
- They play well with others.

Effective pastor search committees are worth their weight in gold. Seek members who possess these traits—whose achievements and leadership experience are matched and marked by their aptitude, wisdom, and character—and you will have a pastor search committee who can bravely guide your church and staff with the highest degree of integrity and insight as you discern whom God is calling to lead your church.

Assign and Delegate Roles and Tasks on Your Committee

With no internal organization, a pastor search committee will lack direction and action. Nothing slows down a pastor search process more than a committee who doesn't know who should be doing what or when.

The first and most important role you need to assign is the search committee chair. Select someone who is a strong and collaborative leader to be the chairperson. This should be someone who has the respect of the other search committee members and someone who has some level of administrative gifts that enables them to facilitate the meetings.

Once the search committee chair has been chosen, the following roles/responsibilities need to be assigned (some of these responsibilities can be shared, and some committee members may be able to take on more than one role):

- Someone organizationally gifted to coordinate meetings and schedules, create the meeting agendas, take meeting minutes, and distribute all notes after each meeting

- Someone who is a great communicator to head up the search committee's communication with the elders, board, congregation, etc.
- Someone who will serve as the prayer coordinator
- Someone who will be the point person for incoming applications and communicating with the applicants
- Someone who will serve as a researcher/recruiter and reach out to candidates your committee finds
- Someone with the gift of hospitality to plan for and entertain the candidates who come in for interviews—pick them up from the airport, show them around, take them to dinner, etc.

Determine How Your Committee Will Make Decisions

Once you know how your church makes decisions, you need to determine how your search committee will make decisions. When you vote on candidates (or any decision you make), will you require a unanimous, consensus, or majority vote? It's important to establish this at the outset of the search process.

A unanimous vote requires all members to be in strong agreement. A consensus vote means that everyone consents to the decision, even if it is not the decision of his or her choice. A majority vote means simply that the majority of votes wins. If you opt for a majority vote, then you must establish how much of a majority a vote must have to pass (90% majority, 75%, two-thirds, 60%, etc.).

Decide How Often, How Much, and How the Committee Will Communicate with the Board/Elders/Congregation, etc.

Once your search committee is formed, it's vital that the committee is aligned with the decision makers of the church, be those the elders, board, staff, congregation, etc. The search committee needs to be on the same page as those responsible for the strategic direction and spiritual health of the church with regard to the needs of the church, the vision and future of the church, and the kind of person who is needed for the next season of ministry.

Having open communication about the search process with both the decision makers of the church and with your church body is of the utmost importance. Make sure that the person appointed to head up the communication of the search committee—whether that is the committee chair or someone else—sets up a schedule of regular and open communication with the congregation, keeping them abreast of what is going on in the process and what they can be praying for. Create a plan for communicating with the congregation throughout the process. We suggest monthly updates either during church services or via e-mail. Include specific prayer requests regarding the search on your website, during announcements, and/or in the bulletin if you use one. Organize quarterly or bimonthly prayer meetings/worship services to bring the congregation together to pray for their next pastor and the discernment of the search committee.

Equip and Train the Committee

Decide what books and articles your pastor search committee will read together. There are wonderful resources available about church leadership, direction, and interviewing candidates—all of which would be extremely helpful for your committee members. Is there any equipping and training that would be valuable for you all to attain together?

Many effective pastor search committees find it valuable to take a retreat together at the outset of the search process. A retreat is a strategic time to seek God's direction in prayer, formulate your search committee's mission, gain clarity on the direction of your church and what you are looking for in a candidate, assign the committee members' roles and responsibilities, brainstorm on places and ways to search, and establish your search time line and committee meeting schedule. Some churches even have a commissioning service to pray for the committee and its direction. (See Appendix C for retreat agenda.)

Thoughts on Confidentiality

It is vital to establish confidentiality guidelines at the very outset of the pastor search process. Protecting the confidentiality of your candidates is good stewardship of the resources God has gifted you with. Never reveal a candidate's name, role, or contact information outside of your search committee until you have hired that person. Do not do anything to jeopardize their position with their current employer. Never contact a candidate's references or conduct any kind of background check until you have their written permission to do so. Being extremely cautious with the confidentiality of your candidates will ultimately build trust with them.

Finding your church's next pastor is a weighty and holy responsibility. Regardless of your church's polity, intentional formation of your search committee is the foundation of an effective pastoral search. And no matter the size of your church or the type of polity that governs it, the search committee will functionally be the group that is selecting your next pastor. Understanding that on the front end is key to prayerfully determining who should be on that committee.

Just like any team or organization, it's vital to have the right people in the right seats. Additionally, a clear purpose, vision, and direction for the pastoral search committee will help align the team toward discerning whom God has called rather than chase personal agendas or politics. With the right people in place headed toward an aligned vision, your search committee will be able to navigate the search process much more gracefully.

Chapter 5

THE PASTOR SEARCH PROCESS

Once you have selected the members of your pastor search committee and determined how you will make decisions, it is time to begin the pastor search process. This can often be the most overwhelming part of the search process as committee members ask, "How do we begin?"

The first step is to establish clear expectations among the search committee as to what to expect in the church's search for a new pastor.

Time Line

While pastoral search is a spiritual endeavor and God will time it, you do need a calendar. Worship is a spiritual endeavor; but amazingly, the services at most churches are exactly the same time each week and have a schedule. God is a planner, and He loves it when we prayerfully plan for the church; so have a schedule in place and leave room for deviation as the Lord leads. Key points in your search to outline:

- How long will you seek input from the congregation about a job description?
- When will the final job description be done?
- How long will you accept résumés?
- When will first phone/virtual interviews be completed?
- When will the first in-person interviews happen?
- When will an offer be extended?

Begin planning with the end in mind. Think about a great time to have a new pastor on board and back your schedule out from there.

Without outside help, it takes the church an average of eighteen to twenty-four months to find a pastor on its own. During this time, churches often lose momentum, giving, and vision. With our process helping search committees walk through the pastor search process, the average time is nine to twelve months. It is vital that the search committee discuss their expectations regarding the time line of the search.

> Without outside help, it takes the church an average of eighteen to twenty-four months to find a pastor on its own.

Costs Involved

Regardless of whether your search committee uses an executive search firm or conducts the search independently, there are costs involved in a pastoral search.

Time: How much time is each search committee member devoting to the search? Is there an expectation for weekly or monthly meetings? How long will these meetings be? Time is expensive, so be sure your committee is in agreement for how much each individual is expected to commit to the process.

Travel: Whether you are flying candidates to come see you or the search committee is flying to see the candidate, there are travel costs involved in the search process. Your search committee needs to have a budget for travel when it comes time to interview candidates.

Hosting—Meals and Accommodations: Will the search committee be having meals together during the meetings? Will the search committee be having meals with the candidates during the interview process? Have a budget outlined for hosting candidates with both meals and accommodations.

Advertising: If your church is planning on advertising the position through job boards or through online networks, do research on what it is going to cost and put it in your budget.

The Process

The Pre-Search Phase

The pre-search phase is foundational to an effective search process. Many search committees feel such an urgency to fill the pulpit that they rush to start finding candidates and evaluating résumés before they have established their committee's roles, direction, communication plan, and job description.

I receive many calls from committee members who are a year or more down the road in their search, frustrated and tired from spinning their wheels with little to no direction because they failed to lay the foundational work in the pre-search phase of the search process.

Here are the steps your search committee needs to take in the pre-search phase.

1. ASSIGN THE ROLES OF EACH SEARCH COMMITTEE MEMBER

A search committee without direction is an unproductive search committee. When committee members don't have direction or ownership over their role on the committee, confusion and tension often sets in. Assigning your committee members a specific role can help dissipate potential tension.

This is especially important for a large committee. One of our clients is a church of 250 located on the North Shore of Chicago. For their Senior Pastor search, they assigned each of their twelve committee members a role for their search process. The two committee co-chairs took responsibility for communicating updates to our team on behalf of the search committee. Two other committee members were responsible for communicating search updates to the congregation on behalf of the committee. Tom, another team member, was the main point of contact between the committee and final candidates. A few other committee members took ownership of writing, producing, and organizing all documentation for the search committee. Their proactive role assignments enabled the committee to be unified in direction as they proceeded through their search. In the end, they were able to find their pastor in only seven months.

The average time it takes for a church to replace its pastor without outside help is twelve to twenty-four months. During this time, churches often experience a loss of momentum, decrease in attendance, and stagnant or decreased giving.

In chapter 4, the roles needed in an effective pastor search committee were listed. In its first meeting, the pastor search committee should assign the roles of each committee member. Ensure that each member of the search committee is 100-percent clear on what his or her responsibility is on the team.

2. ESTABLISH THE PASTOR SEARCH COMMITTEE'S MISSION, VISION, VALUES, AND GOALS

Once each member is clear on his or her role within the committee, establish the committee's mission, vision, values, and goals. This doesn't need to be anything complex, but it should align with the church's overall mission and vision.

We discussed the details of defining your committee's own mission, vision, values, and goals in chapter 4. This is also the perfect time to sign the search committee covenant that we also discussed in chapter 4. Search committees that take the time for this crucial step are far more effective than those that do not.

3. COMPOSE YOUR COMMUNICATION PLAN

Your search committee must decide what communication it is going to share with the congregation and when. We discussed this in detail in chapter 4. One of the biggest tension points churches have is miscommunication or lack of communication between the committee, the church staff, and the congregation. A communication plan minimizes the risk of this tension.

4. CREATE THE JOB DESCRIPTION

Composing and refining the job description is vital to a successful search. Do not simply find a template online. Your job description should be a pastoral profile tailored specifically to your church's culture and the unique characteristics you are looking for your pastor to bring to the role. We will discuss how to develop a job description and pastor profile in detail in chapter 6. You will also find a job description outline in Appendix I.

The Search Phase

Once the search committee has laid the foundational work of the pre-search process, it is time to transition into the search phase. The search phase includes identifying internal candidates, advertising the vacancy, recruiting candidates, and the preliminary screening process.

1. Internal search

Before you begin looking outside your church, take some time to evaluate if there is anyone currently on staff or in a leadership role that should be considered for the position. If there is someone internal who is a viable candidate, do not stop there. It is helpful for both the candidate and the church as a whole to evaluate several candidates, both internal and external, to ensure the right fit.

One of our church clients in southern California was searching for an Assistant Pastor who would oversee discipleship responsibilities. They had an internal candidate who had a relationship with the staff and interviewed well for the role. However, this candidate was the only person they had considered. They wanted our help in expanding their reach and identifying whether the person was the right fit for the role. After a thorough search process and interviewing multiple candidates, they did end up hiring the internal candidate. They had peace of mind that the internal candidate was a great fit after their due diligence in interviewing multiple viable candidates. This is a valuable lesson for search committees. Do not overlook internal candidates. Then, intentionally evaluate them along with viable external candidates to help your committee discern the right fit for your church.

2. Advertising

Only begin advertising during the search phase after the committee has gone through the pre-search phase. Too many times we see searches and even churches fall apart over miscommunication concerning the search. Be sure the committee has properly communicated with the appropriate channels before publicly advertising the role.

3. Recruiting

Recruiting for ministry roles is a delicate process and one that must be handled with care. Pastors are looking for alignment in calling in a role, so it is vital that the recruiting process reflect the guidance of the Holy Spirit.

4. Initial screening

Once you have a pool of viable candidates, it is time for the committee to begin the initial screening process. Remember that you are considering a person with a story and a history, and a résumé is only a small reflection of that person's story. We discuss the importance of looking beyond the résumé in chapter 7.

The Interview Phase

The interview phase is often the most exciting part of the search process for search committees. After several weeks of the pre-search and search phases, it is time for pastor search committees to begin getting to know candidates.

1. Phone interview

After an initial screening of the candidates, it is time for the committee to begin conversations with the candidates. A best practice is to begin with a phone interview rather than a video interview. This might seem counterintuitive in the twenty-first century; but more often than not, technological issues prohibit video interviews from being as effective as anticipated and can leave both the candidate and the interviewer frustrated. Your search committee might decide to do multiple phone interviews depending on how many candidates you are considering. The primary focus of these interviews should be competency and basic theological alignment.

Never hire someone solely based on a phone or video interview. I learned this lesson when I started helping churches with staffing. I had several committees ask if I could interview candidates virtually—over the phone or by video—in an effort to save on travel costs.

We love technology and leverage it wherever we can. We also loved the idea of building something more cost effective that would allow more churches to use a search firm in their process. So we built a "virtual search" process. We used the same people, the same process, the same database, and the same interviewing techniques. The only difference was we cut out travel and face-to-face meetings and replaced them with virtual meetings.

The results were not the same. Our client satisfaction rate (and success rate) when doing our full, face-to-face process had been about 98 percent. When we started offering virtual search, it dropped to about 65 percent (for those using virtual). The success rates of hiring dropped. The length of tenure for those hired dropped. In short, everything dropped to about a 50/50 gamble on success. What seemed like a practical way to save money and leverage new technology turned out to be a miserable failure.

We stopped offering the virtual service because we quickly realized that nothing could replace the value of sitting face-to-face, knee-to-knee with a candidate to discuss his call to ministry, his marriage, how they raise their kids, qualifications for their role, and chemistry with the church staff. You can't read body language over phone or video, which is crucial to the interview process. People are fearfully and wonderfully made. They are complex. They are messy. And sizing them up as your potential pastor requires seeing them in person.

Virtual interviews have a place in the search process but cannot be the sole interview for hiring. Unless the job is going to be done virtually or over the phone, the final interview cannot be virtual or over the phone.

I often tell people that the big lesson in our failed virtual search is that "if virtual really worked, Jesus would have Skyped in instead of coming down to earth."

So while phone and video interviews can be a helpful starting point, make sure that you never hire someone solely based on a virtual interview.

2. FACE-TO-FACE INTERVIEW

After initial phone interviews, it is time to enter into the face-to-face interview process. The primary focus of these interviews is chemistry fit among the church staff and search committee. It is likely that you will have multiple face-to-face interviews as the pastoral candidate meets with different key decision makers. It is important that both the candidate and the church be clear about confidentiality expectations at this point in the process. See Appendix K for an example of an on-site interview template as a framework for your pastor search committee.

3. Spousal interview

A key component of a successful Senior Pastor search is the involvement of the candidate's spouse. The best pastor search committees understand that they are recruiting and assessing not only the candidate but also the spouse. If the couple is not on the same page regarding a transition, a move, or even a change affecting their family, the search process will fall apart. Spend intentional time with the spouse throughout the search process.

Bring the spouse in early on in the interview process. A church in Arizona was hiring an Associate Pastor. They found a candidate whom they really liked for the role who was in a different state. The church brought in the candidate several times over a four-month period. On the final visit, when they were going to make the candidate a job offer, they invited the candidate's wife in for the first time. It turned out that she did not feel peace about the role or moving their family across the country. This was devastating for the church after investing months of emotional energy and money into interviews with the candidates.

For a pastoral role, it is vital to bring the spouse in for the interview process to ensure that the husband and wife are aligned in their calling to the role and the church community.

The Post-Interview Phase

1. REFERENCE AND BACKGROUND CHECKS

One of the biggest mistakes you can make in your hiring process is skipping the background and reference checks on your potential hire. A reference check is your opportunity to protect your church and learn how best to lead your potential hire from people who have done so in the past. A thorough background check includes a credit, criminal, education, and reference check.

A misconception about conducting church background checks is that they are intended to "dig up dirt" on a potential hire. This is not the case. The process of conducting church background checks is intended for you to (a) make sure that the candidate is who he says he is and (b) allow you to get to know your potential new team member better and gain clarity on whether they would be a good fit for your team or not.

2. OFFER LETTER

The offer letter should be personal yet professional. It should clearly outline the position for which you are hiring, the compensation structure, housing allowance, insurance overview, and any benefits included in the package.

3. LETTING CANDIDATES GO

Navigating the steps to hiring the right addition to your church staff can take a lot of work. Much time is spent on determining if they have the right mix of experience, personality, theology, etc. Because of this extensive effort and focus, it can be difficult to know how to deal with the "other" candidates—the ones who are good at what they do, whom you've interviewed or called, but who just aren't the right fit for your church staff. How should church leaders let good candidates go in an honorable and godly way?

4. Provide Closure and Give Constructive Feedback

This one should be a no-brainer, but I can tell you from firsthand experience that it is not. Church leaders can be so focused on finding someone to say yes to that they forget to say no. Make a phone call or send an e-mail to candidates as soon as it has been determined that they aren't going to move forward. Despite the momentary disappointment, most candidates find it a great relief when they hear that a door has closed. With every pastor search we complete, e-mails and phone calls go out to every candidate who has applied as a way of closing the door and thanking candidates for trusting us with the process. If your church has had a phone conversation or a face-to-face interaction with a candidate, at the very least an e-mail is an appropriate way to inform them that the church is continuing to search elsewhere. Especially if a candidate has been interviewed in person, it is extremely helpful to the candidate if they are given feedback on themselves. As much as we try to know ourselves, hearing an evaluation from a new source can be eye-opening and can help a candidate better present themselves the next time. Also, this is a great exercise for church leaders as well because it allows them to articulate more what they desire in the final candidate. It might be revealing to go through this exercise only to find that the search committee was approaching the candidates with unrealistic expectations.

What to Do When You're Stuck

Are you fishing with the wrong lure? If you have let all your candidates go, it is time for some reflection on what you are looking for. Consider refining your job description or even job title in order to attract the right candidates to the opening on your church staff. If you are working with an executive search firm, make sure to provide feedback to them as well.

A church in the Central Valley of California launched their pastor search a couple of months before they changed the name of the church and rebranded. During this rebranding, the search committee realized that some of the Teaching Pastor role qualifications they were looking for had changed as their church had a renewed vision for their future. They reflected as a team on what had changed and then documented the changes that the search committee agreed upon in a new job description. Each member of the search committee signed the document to ensure they were aligned in the search moving forward.

Clarity is key to an effective search process, so be sure continually to evaluate if the search committee is clear on what they are looking for as you continue through the search process.

Onboarding

An intentional onboarding process is vital to the long-term success of your new pastor. High-capacity pastors will want to spend the first few days meeting new team members, learning the staff culture, and asking a lot of questions. The most effective churches have an onboarding system in place for the first couple of weeks that allows the pastor time to observe, build relationships, and learn the culture before making any changes. We'll cover specifics on effective onboarding in chapter 9.

Leading the pastor search process is hard work and is an immense responsibility. If you apply this process framework, you'll be well on your way to a successful search.

As we near the end of this chapter on process, I want to draw your attention to thirteen common mistakes that I've seen pastor search committees make too often.

Common Mistakes of Pastor Search Committees

1. Have unrealistic expectations. Do you expect that your new pastor is going to be exactly like your former pastor? Do you think your final candidate will check off every box on your wish list? Do you know the differences between the attributes you want and the ones you really need in your next pastor? Be realistic in your expectations about your next pastor.

2. Don't manage the expectations of the church. Does your congregation expect that the new pastor is going to be able to fix all your problems? Use the Pastor Search Committee

Prayer Calendar in Appendix A to assist your congregation in praying through your search.

3. Have too many people involved in the decision process. There's a lot of truth to the phrase, "Too many cooks in the kitchen." It's also very important to make sure that your pastor search committee members don't have an agenda. If a decision maker is insisting on their own agenda throughout the Senior Pastor search, it will constantly stall and muddy the process.

4. Disagree with one another. Whether or not you're using a search firm to help you find your next Senior Pastor, the decision makers for the search (search committee, elders, board, etc.) need to have clarity and agreement on what they are looking for before beginning to evaluate and interview candidates.

5. Have unproductive and disorganized meetings. If you don't have a clear time line for your Senior Pastor search, detailed agendas for your meetings, and specific roles for your committee members, you're sure to have an unproductive, disorganized, and frustrating search process (which candidates will most likely pick up on).

6. Be closed off to anyone different from your previous pastor. If you want exactly what you had last time and if you aren't open to any differences, you will always be disappointed. You'll also discourage and scare away your potential candidates who cannot possibly meet your expectations.

7. Don't involve the spouse of the candidate in the interview process. This caveat is twofold. First, a candidate's spouse may not be completely on board with the new job prospect if your church overlooks or ignores them during the interview. Make sure the spouse knows how welcomed they would be as well. Second, too often we've seen churches hire a pastor without interviewing their spouse, only to find marriage issues or job conflicts later. For this reason, when we conduct Senior Pastor searches, our Executive Search Consultants interview the final candidate's spouse as well.

8. Be overly invasive in the interview process and the background search. Remember that the interview process is part of building your relationship with your potential new Senior Pastor. Background and reference checks are vitally important, but if you come across as overly invasive like hiring a private investigator to secretly stalk your candidate, you might be setting up that relationship on a foundation of distrust.

9. Take too long with the interview process. It's important to note that your Senior Pastor candidate is interviewing you as well. If you take too long to communicate with him, bring him in for interviews, or make decisions, that will be indicative to the interviewing pastor of the way your church makes decisions and might make them rethink the position.

10. Judge candidates by their preaching videos alone. When you judge candidates solely by their sample teaching videos, you're not always taking into account the context and setting of those videos. Remember that it's vital to have a balance of shepherding and teaching attributes in your Senior Pastor, and you can't always see those shepherding and discipling strengths in a candidate's preaching sample video.

11. Put too much emphasis on a particular style of preaching. If you're set on one specific style of preaching, you may rule out a lot of high-capacity candidates. Biblical preaching should be the goal, not a particular style.

12. Surprise your candidates late in the interview process. As I mentioned before, if you aren't completely honest with your candidates from the beginning of the interview process, you build your relationship with your potential Senior Pastor on a foundation of mistrust. For example, if you sweep all the dirt under the rug at first and then during the late stages of the interview process disclose that the church is in a lot of debt or that there is unrest among your staff, you have a high risk of losing that candidate. Be open and honest about the church and your situation from day one, and your candidates will trust you.

13. Don't follow through with promises you made during the interview process. Don't over-promise things to candidates that you aren't willing to make reality once they're in their new position. If you put a lot of limits on the changes that the Senior Pastor can make after they've begun pastoring your church, you may find yourself looking for a new Senior Pastor sooner than you'd like.

Use this process framework and avoid these mistakes during your pastor search, and your search committee will be on its way to a smooth search process as you seek the Lord regarding the one whom He is calling to your church.

Chapter 6

KNOW YOUR CHURCH

Paramount to the success of the pastoral search process is knowing your church. The church's mission, vision, values, organizational structure, and long-term growth strategy are all determining factors of the type of candidate your church needs. It is then not enough just to know your church. You must be able to enunciate all of the aspects that contribute to your church's character in a way that attracts the proper potential pastoral candidates. This chapter will help pastor search committees shape their church profile, job description, and key results areas for the role.

Mission, Vision, and Values

The first step in knowing your church so that the pastoral search committee can accurately and attractively portray your church to potential candidates is to enunciate your church's mission, vision, and values.

Your church likely already has a mission statement and an idea of vision and values, but are they all written down? If they're all already written down, consider revisiting them. During a season of transition, thinking and talking through where you've been, where you're going, how you're going to get there, and what you believe in can be not only helpful but healing.

> During a season of transition, thinking and talking through where you've been, where you're going, how you're going to get there, and what you believe in can be not only helpful but healing.

Begin this process by working with your pastor search committee as well as your elder board to visit your existing mission statement, any statement of vision or annual report that casts vision, and list of values you may have. I caution you to not think of this as simply rebranding your church (not that that is a bad thing to do), but to dive much deeper, examining each piece in turn and determining its relevance and how well it aligns with the current and future states of your church.

Your Mission Statement

Your mission statement is your way of telling the community what your church is passionate about. It shouldn't be something that was thrown together or something crafted simply for mass appeal. There is great power in it. Your mission statement is something that should guide your ministries, your projects, and your community outreach.

There are many resources available for crafting mission statements—some for the corporate world and some for the faith-based world. This chapter is not meant to be an all-inclusive guide to mission statement writing or in any way to replace any of those resources. Rather, I simply want to communicate the gravity that a mission statement can have.

In thinking and, more importantly, praying through your mission statement with your search committee members and elder board, consider what it would look like for your church to be "on mission" and "off mission."

We hear "off mission" when a mistake has already been made. Start with crafting a mission statement that captures the true spirit of your church's mission succinctly and you'll be well on your way to knowing your church well enough to communicate it to others and motivate them to join your team.

Your Vision

In this time of transition, it is especially important to remain focused on the future. Your vision for the future is one of the best ways to discern what kind of candidate you need to hire. Beyond just reviewing a résumé and teaching samples, your church needs a pastor whose vision truly aligns with that of your church.

Times of transition, sadly, can also mean times of shock, of sadness, of confusion. That is to say that most of the time during a pastoral transition in a church, the congregation and the elder board are usually worried first and foremost with the current state of the church. Many times, everyone is in a season of mourning the loss of the pastor. Sometimes the congregation may feel disillusioned, especially if the transition is a result of a moral failure. Though spirits may be low and though people may be distracted, it is important to evaluate the church's vision for the future now more than ever.

Look to the chair of the pastor search committee or a well-respected elder to rally around the church's vision. Pray through the vision intensely, asking God for clarity, for healing, and for wisdom. During the meeting or meetings that go into discussing vision, do your best as a group not to linger on the possible past sadness, but to look forward.

Determining your vision for the future of the church is a part of the pastor search process that can bring great healing where it is greatly needed.

For the technical part of the vision, assess the mission statement that your search committee has already talked and prayed through. Based on that mission statement, where do you see the church going after the new pastor is in place? What are the logical next steps for your various ministries? In what ways would your new pastor effectively lead your congregation toward achieving that vision? It is of the utmost importance during the technical phase of the vision that the pastor search committee and the elder board be realistic in their vision. If the apostle Paul wouldn't be able to achieve your vision, you're likely aiming too high.

Your Values

Perhaps the most significant impact on your church's day-to-day operations and work culture is made by your values.

Oftentimes in the church world, broad claims are made and accepted as values that have little effect on the actual culture of the work environment and character of the worship services.

Our team has nine values that guide everything we do. We infuse these values into every step of our process from staff meetings to consulting with the pastor search committees with which we are working.

Coming to these values didn't happen overnight. We took several months of brainstorming and refining before we finalized and documented them. We first brought our entire team together and asked, "What are words or phrases that describe the way we approach our work?" We then narrowed them down as we streamlined and eliminated overlap among the initial ideas. After that, we took several months to pray over them. We then added phrases to describe how our team lives out each value and documented them so that our entire team was on the same page about how our work would reflect each value. They are:

1. BROADBAND LOVE

We're a company built on the values of our Christian faith. As a company, we endeavor to live in grace and walk in love. We strive to show love to each client and candidate with whom we interact.

2. UNUSUAL SERVANTHOOD

We exist to serve our clients and candidates in a way that makes them say, "I've never been treated like that by a company."

3. Wow-making excellence

We can't promise to be all things to all people, but we can strive to be all things to our clients. We endeavor to under-promise and over-deliver through each step of the search process. We also work to be a thought leader in the search industry, creating top-notch articles and resources to help organizations follow staffing and leadership best practices.

4. Ridiculous responsiveness

In the world of smart phones, the world is at our fingertips. Quality comes first, but speed comes next. We want to deliver quality service at lightning speed.

5. Solution-side living

The Vanderbloemen team members are problem solvers, always having a solution mentality and not a victim mentality.

6. Ever-increasing agility

Being flexible is too rigid. We strive for agility to serve our clients and candidates with excellence in an ever-changing marketplace. Each employee at Vanderbloemen has "other duties as required" built into their job description.

7. Stewardship of life

We measure success on our ability to maintain personal and corporate financial, spiritual, physical, and vocational boundaries. Each employee is required to give charitably of his or her time, talent, and resources.

8. CONSTANT IMPROVEMENT

Vanderbloemen Search Group strives for *kaizen*, the Japanese business philosophy of continuous improvement of working practices and personal efficiency. Each Vanderbloemen employee has an insatiable curiosity for making systems and processes better. The marketplace is changing daily, and Vanderbloemen Search Group strives to stay ahead of the curve by constantly asking, "How can we improve?"

9. CONTAGIOUS FUN

We take our work seriously but not ourselves. Vanderbloemen loves what we do, and our joy for helping our clients is contagious. You'll often find us at a local restaurant enjoying each other's company after work hours, because we genuinely like each other.

Once we put our values into words, we didn't just put those in a file for future generations to return to, but rather memorialized them on coasters that sit on everyone's desk. Every week during our staff meeting, one person on our team talks about the way they've seen one or more of our values lived out on our team. What would your values be if you intentionally went through and enunciated them?

Every organization's values are going to look different. The key to effective values is to make them specific, meaningful, and actionable. If your church is just starting out in thinking about what your values should be, you might find it helpful to start with the fruits of the Spirit in Galatians 5:23–24.

Once you have your values written down, your culture will become much more apparent. During a time of transition, these concrete values can remind you what you stand for as a church as well as what to look for in a candidate. Interviewing a candidate based on how well he fits with your values is just another step to ensuring a great fit.

Avoid Hiring Aspirationally

Many churches fall into the trap of hiring the person they wish would be good for the church rather than the one who really is a fit for the church. I cannot count the times that a search committee has hired (or called) a pastor so that they can bring a lot of "new young families" into the church only to realize a few years into the pastorate that the church is not ready for the change (and the pain that comes with change) that is needed to reach those new young families. There is a graveyard miles long of short-term pastors who were told one set of goals by the search committee only to find that the reality in the larger church was much different.

As you get to know your church, even beyond mission, vision, and values, be sure you know what kind of pastor will fit your church, not just what your church says they need. Take the pulse of the church through surveys. Take a long look at how much change the church has historically been able to tolerate. That's a pretty good indicator of what they will be able to tolerate going forward. Hiring based on who you are as a church rather than who you wish you were may make the difference between a long, fruitful pastorate and a short-lived failure.

Bring Someone in from Outside the Church

Many churches fall into the trap of lacking an objective third party in the crucial process of hiring their next senior leader. No matter the situation, when a group of people from the same organization gets together under the same circumstances, there is a natural lack of outside perspective. It is quite difficult, if not impossible, to take an accurate and comprehensive look at the state of an organization if you are a part of it. For that reason, consider bringing in an outside consultant. An outside consultant has the benefit of not having an agenda as well as having expertise in helping hundreds of churches build successful teams.

The role of the outside consultant will be to take an objective pulse of the church as a whole. The consultant can guide you through discussions of mission, vision, and values as well as evaluate the makeup of the team. How effective is the church staff in its current structure? The lay leaders? The search committee? It's much better to have someone come in with an objective perspective and not be swayed by what they want to see. This will help ensure you are setting up your church on a healthy foundation as you begin the process of searching for your next senior leader

The consultant can help sort through the bylaws and how they relate to your mission, vision, and values so that any

needed changes can be made before you start your search process. It is often the outside consultant who is able to point out
the major blind spots of the congregation before it's too late.

Bring in an Interim Pastor

In our work with churches during transition times, we've
found that it is often helpful to bring in an interim pastor. It
is particularly important that this person have an agreement
not to become the lead pastor so that they can stay objective
throughout the process. Beyond helping with the teaching and
the day-to-day operations, an interim pastor can offer a unique
viewpoint on your staff; the elder board; the pastor search committee; the congregation; and the state of your mission, vision,
and values.

A major benefit of having someone come in as an interim
pastor is the amount of exposure that they have to your search
committee, your congregation, your staff, and your elder board.
They are able to get a sense of exactly how everyone is living
out your mission, vision, and values. The interim pastor can
help detect blind spots that none of the committee members or
staff have seen.

Many churches are, at first, concerned with the idea of
bringing in an interim pastor, thinking that it's a practice
that comes from the corporate world and has no place in the
realm of the church. Other churches worry that bringing in an
interim pastor is just one more change that the congregation
will have to endure. What these churches find, however, is that

an effective interim pastor is able to take the wheel of the ship in troubled times and steer it out of the storm. There are many interim pastors specifically gifted and called to serve churches in this way.

If you decide to bring on an interim pastor, make sure to set expectations with him before he ever comes on staff. Set out a time line for time with your staff and specific goals that he will help you accomplish while he is there. Have him be intentional about assessing your mission, vision, and values so that they'll be able to thoughtfully and prayerfully produce a document with their findings. Some interim pastors are gifted in systems and therefore able to assess easily the effectiveness of your staff or the implementation of your mission, vision, and values. Setting expectations will help ensure that you and your church healthily navigate out of your season of transition.

Creating Buy-In Among the Church Community

During a transition, many search committees and elder boards worry about the congregation and how they will react to the pastor search process. They worry that they will not like the candidate they select, that people will leave if the church changes drastically, and that they'll leave if the process takes too long.

What we've seen in our work with churches in times of transition is that congregations are most negatively affected by feeling that they don't have a say in the process. Most people in the congregations we work with don't want to be on the search committee as much as they want to be heard by the search committee. While we've already walked through the appropriate methods to communicate with your congregation during the pastor search process, there are many ways to connect with your congregation during this time of reflecting on the spirit and character of the church.

One interesting way to reach out to your congregation during the pastor search process is to take a congregational survey. Beyond the feeling of ownership that it gives the congregation, the congregational survey is a tool that can bring in useful information about the congregation's needs, their demographics, and their sense of community or ownership of the church.

A survey that we've seen handed out to congregations by pastor search committees is one that outlines the three roles of a pastor according to the primary "offices of Christ" as outlined in Reformed theology. Those "offices" describe the primary functions (or job descriptions) that Jesus filled and are formally labeled as Jesus: Prophet, Priest, and King. The survey outlines the role of each. Translated into pastoral offices, the pastoral job is segmented into the following: "Can the pastor communicate the Word to us?" (Prophet); "Can the pastor minister to us?" (Priest); and "Can the pastor run the organization of our church?" (King).

The King is gifted in the ability to rule. He "makes the trains run on time." The Prophet has great vision and voice. He is the gifted preacher and teacher. The Priest is the one gifted with a pastoral heart. He has a great bedside manner, a heart for people and for interpersonal communication. Once you communicate what each of these pastoral roles are, have each member of the congregation circle the one (and they can only circle one) that they most look for in a pastor. The results of this survey will likely come back revealing that the congregation wants a good speaker and a man with a pastoral heart. However, if you surveyed the elder board, staff, or pastor search committee you might come up with something much different.

An interesting and sometimes confounding aspect of surveys is that they are only able to reveal useful information if they are carefully crafted. Many surveys, like the one mentioned above, have a good intention but miss the mark because they survey a group that has very little exposure and knowledge of only one piece of the survey.

When crafting a survey that truly will be useful to your pastor search committee, use a thoughtful mix of questions targeted at demographic information, spiritual information, and impressions of the church. Demographics and spiritual background are great metrics for predicting what kind of candidate would be successful.

In addition to the content of the questions, keep in mind the tact behind them. Consider attempting to elicit the information from your congregation regarding what topics they'd like to hear preached about. Instead of asking that question bluntly, try: "If you were bringing a friend or loved one who does not yet know Christ to a service, what type of message do you think would reach them?" Another question that can help bring out valuable information is: "What is your faith background?" The answers to this question can give you a pulse of where your congregation is coming from theologically. In the same vein, the question "Where did you come to know Christ?" can reveal how deeply connected your congregation is to your church. If they came to know Christ in your church, it's likely they feel a great deal of ownership of it.

Last, you should always keep in mind that survey results really need to be interpreted and not taken at face value. Surveys can only tell you so much and should be used as a means to inform and only gently guide the search process rather than as hard and fast tools for disqualifying candidates. The mere act of surveying can communicate to the congregation that they have a stake in the future and vision of the church, but the implications of the results of the survey should be heavily interpreted before use.

Job Description for Your Pastor Profile

Once you and your pastor search committee, elder board, and staff have poured through the research you've done and worked to enunciate your mission, vision, and values as well as taken the pulse of your congregation and prayerfully committed to the search process, you'll be equipped to begin the process of crafting a job description. A job description is the document that will aid your search committee or the search firm you hire to advertise that particular role and discuss the expectations of the role with potential candidates. See

Appendix I for specific details that should be included in your job description/pastor profile.

Before writing the job description, however, you must know who is responsible for its content. Is this a document that is authored by the pastor search committee and then approved by the elder board? Is the document solely written by the elder board? Or is the document a collaborative effort? One effective way this can be done is to have the pastor search committee work with the outside consultant, search firm, and interim pastor to draft the document, then have it blessed by the elder board. At this point in the process, it is especially important to work with either an outside consultant or search firm as a guide so that you include all the necessary responsibilities of the role with the appropriate language so that the search process can be truly streamlined. Many times, pastor search committees will use their own internal language rather than that of the current job market. This can lead to confusion in prospective candidates, make the job seem unattractive, or mislead candidates. Having an unbiased third party who has knowledge of the pastor search process will help to ensure that your pastor search committee produces a clear job description that accurately communicates the role and the spirit of your church while properly managing expectations.

The question then is: "So what do we include in the job description?" There are pieces both technical and spiritual that you should include. First, what will be the realistic responsibilities of your new pastor? Look at all of the information you've collected so far to start putting this information together.

What teams will they lead? What are your expectations for teaching? For missions? Your staff structure will help inform this piece of the job description. A consultant's notes or those of an interim pastor will be especially helpful with this part of the job description. If you're a smaller church, your pastor will likely need to wear several hats, so enunciate those here.

One important note on the technical piece of the job description: be realistic. A pastor (and human) can only shoulder so much responsibility and accomplish so much. Make sure you're balancing the requirements of the role with the abilities of a human being.

Once the technical portion of the job description is complete, look to the spiritual. The tendency in this portion is to try to cover all of your bases spiritually. Instead of copying whole passages of Scripture here, remember that the purpose of this document is to communicate briefly to prospective candidates what the role of pastor at your particular church means. Your pastor should champion your values, so build these into this piece of the job description. He should also have passions that align with the mission and vision of your church. What are those? Should he have a heart for missions? For caring for the broken here at home? For reaching those who have turned away from or been hurt by the church? Whatever your passion is as a church, make that apparent in the job description.

Finally, it's important to include "all other duties as required" on every job description. It's impossible to predict everything the pastor of your church may need to do. It is also important that any candidate for the role of pastor be ready and willing to roll up their sleeves and get to the task, whether that be baptizing, leading a team that has no leader, or washing feet.

While not in the job description, it is important that the search committee know what "other duties as necessary" means. If there is a death in the church, is the pastor expected to be at the hospital at 3 a.m. on Saturday night? How many weddings a year should the pastor be expected to perform? If the alarm goes off at the church on a Friday night, is the pastor expected to be the point of contact? Whatever the size of your church, be sure to ask these questions or whatever is appropriate to your setting to have a clear understanding of what a pastor will face when he is in his new role.

Growth Strategy

The final piece of the puzzle when it comes to getting to know your church is its growth strategy. While it sounds businesslike, a growth strategy is a great tool to use alongside your mission, vision, and values statements. In getting to know your church, find whether you have a growth strategy and then whether that growth strategy is still relevant from when it was drafted.

A growth strategy, simply put, is a plan for the growth of the church and what resources will be needed to accomplish it. Every congregation needs a proportional number of staff and volunteers to serve it adequately. As the church grows, the growth strategy is helpful in letting you know when you should make your next hire.

When it comes to finding a new pastor, the growth strategy will help the elder board and pastor search committee know whether the incoming pastor is coming onto a staff that is already lacking and whether there is an adequate number of volunteers. That can also inform what kind of candidate the church needs. If the team is well staffed with both paid staff and volunteers, perhaps a candidate without a strong background of building teams might be worth considering. If the team is lacking, then having a candidate come onboard who has proven experience growing staff and raising up volunteers would be essential.

If your church does not have a growth strategy, hiring an outside consultant or a search firm with experience in building teams can speed the process as well as offer an informed perspective on numbers and best practices.

Chapter 7

KNOW WHO'S OUT THERE

Finding the best candidates out there can feel like the most daunting part of the pastor search process. Having clarity about whom you're looking for is the first place to start.

Defining Reasonable Pastoral Characteristics: Desirables vs. Practicals

When our team comes alongside a church in a senior pastor search, we often come across a divided search committee. This is for various reasons, but more often than not, it's over the lack of clarity regarding whom they are looking for. They have a list of twenty qualities; but none of them are negotiable, and all of them are the number-one priority. While all of us would love our senior pastor to be Jesus (though a more modern version who is married, drives a minivan, and has 2.5 children), there is no perfect candidate out there. Every pastor possesses different strengths, weaknesses, and leadership abilities. The question you need to ask is: Which characteristics are required, and which are preferred?

What are the practical qualities your next Senior Pastor must possess, and what are the desirable qualities on which you can make concessions?

Practical Characteristics

Practicals are the innate traits that are "unteachable." These are built-in inclinations of someone's decision making, response, and drive that influence all of their work. This could also include pure talent.

Here are some helpful pointers to consider as you begin crafting the type of candidate needed for this role:

- What are the characteristics of the ideal candidate for this position that cannot be compromised because they cannot be taught?

This includes the candidate's character, people skills, and natural talents such as integrity and faithfulness.

For example, a certain level of education is always a desirable; but ingenuity, creative thinking, and agility are innate traits that cannot be compromised or taught. Say you review a candidate with demonstrated faithfulness, results, and capacity—it's unwise to immediately discard a candidate based solely upon education credentials.

- Does the candidate have the capacity to get the job done and thrive while doing it? Have they had a demonstrated performance of thriving in a similar setting?

We spend intentional time on these questions because we believe the long-term success of both the candidate and the church depends on the answer to these two questions being a resounding yes.

Desirable Characteristics

Desirables are the characteristics that, if the candidate is perfect in every way, we could consider letting go or consider teaching the candidate once they are a part of the team.

These are some of the questions to be asked as a part of the discovery process:

- How large or small of a background does the church prefer the candidate come from?
- How many years of education and ministry experience does the church prefer the candidate have?
- Must their experience align perfectly with the role in order for the candidate to be successful in this role?
- What is the church's theology? Must the candidate and the church agree on every theological topic?
- What is the church's expectation for sermon delivery? How long should a sermon be? Should it be a line-by-line expository approach to preaching or a topical, series-based approach? Should a pastor address political issues, or stay silent?

The key to these questions is "Does it matter?" They are not meant to devalue the church or the candidate but to evaluate the values of each in order to ensure the right fit.

When a search committee is evaluating a Senior Pastor candidate and dismisses the candidate solely on the quality of their video sermon sample, even when all the innate traits (ability to lead a team, cultivate leaders, and proven record of growth) are there, the search committee could be missing an opportunity to interview an excellent candidate. A candidate is much more than one sermon sample, and sermon style preferences vary from church to church. Try not to let subjective preferences be a hindrance to considering a candidate who has potential to be a great candidate for your church. Style can be taught. However, skill and talent cannot. Be careful not to confuse the two.

If you're reading this chapter in the midst of evaluating candidates, take a moment with your team and review the list of characteristics you desire from your ideal candidate. From that list, categorize them into my two suggested categories: Practicals vs. Desirables. Then next to each one, ask yourself: Is this trait absolutely necessary for the candidate to be successful in this role? Chances are that most of them will be, but there might be one in there that can be bent—and that might be the key to finding the right candidate.

Where to Look for Pastoral Candidates

As you begin to actively look for candidates, be sure to consider all of your options. The key to a successful search is turning over every rock possible to find the one whom God is calling to your church.

These are some of the best places to begin resourcing for possible candidates.

Look Internally

We always encourage our churches to look internally when they are beginning a search. Is there someone currently on staff who has been developed enough to become the new senior leader? We often consult with churches to help them evaluate if an internal candidate is ready to step into the senior leader role.

Look at Sons and Daughters of the Church

Are there members of the church who have gone into ministry? Are there former staff members who could be good candidates? Are there churches like yours (or churches you have planted) that have staff? When doing an organ transplant, doctors look at family members first. Are there members of your extended family who might work as candidates?

Denominational and Network Help

Many churches are still a part of a denomination, and even most nondenominational churches have a network of churches they turn to for help. These are a great resource to begin reaching out to for references of possible candidates.

Guest Speakers

Take inventory over the past few years of guest speakers at your church and reach out to them for referrals as to whom they might know who might be interested in the role.

Area Churches

Are there churches in your area that could be a good resource? Sometimes the best connection is a church that has recently walked through a pastoral transition as well.

Outgoing Senior Pastor

If possible and appropriate, ask your outgoing Senior Pastor for advice and some possible resources. Your Senior Pastor will have a handful of peers who could not only be possible candidates but have connections to others praying through a pastoral transition.

Conferences and Seminars

A good leader is always seeking out continuing education opportunities, so conferences and seminars that are relevant to your church's vision and values may be a helpful resource.

Seminaries

Contact the seminaries within your denomination or theological family for referrals to either recent graduates or alumni they might recommend.

Best Practices for Job Boards and Advertising Job Descriptions

Job Boards

Years ago, putting out an ad for an open staff or pastor position was fairly easy, simply because there were only a few places to post them. Now that the Internet is such a large part of our lives, the world has become more connected. However, this connectedness has also created a lot of noise. There are now so many places to post opportunities online that it can be overwhelming for search committees as they discern which are worth their time and which are not.

Though many churches are hoping to find their next pastor through resources and internal searching, posting on job boards can help build momentum and excitement about your search.

Say what you need to say in 140 characters or less

Like it or not, the social media world is here to stay. And for a number of reasons, pastors have latched onto it like no other group. In fact, a 2012 *New York Times* article stated, "Evangelical Christian leaders whose inspirational messages of God's love perform about 30 times as well as Twitter messages from pop culture powerhouses like Lady Gaga."[1] Someone on your committee should spend a focused amount of time thinking through how to describe your opening in short form, short enough to be posted on Twitter.

Even if you don't use social media, pastors love the "bottom line" description of a job and will be attracted to churches that know how to articulate distinctly what they want in a short amount of space. How would you describe your pastoral opening uniquely, and in 140 characters or less?

Your job description should be a recruiting tool

There is no magic formula to an effective job description. However, it should be written in a way that engages the reader and helps them see a vision for the role. High-capacity candidates will be looking for a mission to join, not just a role to fill.

Here are some questions to ask as you write your job description:

- Is your description attractional while still being true to the character of the church?
- Did you give candidates a description of the community in which your church is ministering?
- Is the description clear, thorough, but still concise?
- Think about the type of pastor you're hoping to draw in. Would this description attract them?
- Do you have a link to your church website on the job description?

It's never been easier to look better

One reality of the Internet age is this: it has never been easier to look better on paper than you do in real life. On the flip side, many pastors have never been taught how to create a résumé, so a great candidate can look horrible on paper. A résumé is helpful but only tells you so much about a candidate. If you find a résumé that interests you, take some time to do a bit of research on the candidate beyond the résumé. It is impossible for one person to be summed up on a piece of paper, so take time to get to know candidates beyond their résumé.

Note

1. Amy O'Leary, "Christian Leaders Are Powerhouses on Twitter," *New York Times*, June 2, 2012, http://www.nytimes.com/2012/06/02 /technology/christian-leaders-are-powerhouses-on-twitter.html?_r=0.

Chapter 8

FIGURE OUT WHO'S A MATCH

Once the search committee has a thorough job description, has publicized the role, recruited candidates, and begun an initial screening, it is time for the search committee to begin the interviewing process. This can be one of the most overwhelming parts of the search process for committee members.

Interviewing Process and Time Line

The interviewing process is an art, not a science. We see many great organizations interview candidates too much before making the decision to hire them, losing the candidate in the meantime. We also see many great organizations move too fast through the interview process and then have to redo the search again because they did not thoroughly vet the candidate.

When you are ready to begin interviewing candidates, we recommend using the following steps as a framework for crafting your own interviewing process. By no means is this applicable to every church's situation, but we hope it's helpful as you begin the interview process.

Step 1: Schedule a phone interview between the candidate and the key stakeholders in the hiring process.

Step 2: Schedule a face-to-face interview between the candidate and the key stakeholders. For Senior Pastor searches, have the spouse come along for the interview. While they do not need to be a part of the entire interview process, involving them early will help provide clarity for both the church and the couple regarding chemistry fit among the church community and the couple.

Step 3: Have key stakeholders visit the pastor's current church to see how he shepherds his current congregation. It is important that the search committee respect the candidate's confidentiality during this part of the process, if applicable.

Step 4: Bring the candidate and spouse back out to the church for a final interview. Depending on the church's polity, this might be the time when the pastor is coming in view of a call or when the church has the pastor preach from the pulpit. That will depend on the church, but this interview should only happen if the church is highly considering making an offer to the candidate. This might also be the time when the pastor and spouse meet with different groups within the church to build relationships and answer questions.

Video Interviewing

While video conference technology is improving by the day, we do not recommend that your first impression of a candidate come from a video interview. It never fails that one party's Internet will experience issues, causing frustration during the video interview. Start with a phone interview and then follow with a video interview if necessary. However, we always recommend that interviews be done face-to-face as much as possible.

The Art of Interviewing for Ministry

There is no other vocation that so intimately intertwines one's spiritual, emotional, and professional being as ministry. This fact makes the interviewing process an art, as pastor search committees are evaluating emotional and spiritual health along with competency and cultural fit for the role.

Theological values also make interviewing for ministry complex. A church in Washington State had a difficult feat in their pastor search, as they were looking for a specific theological match in addition to chemistry fit. The church adhered to a Reformed but dispensational theology, which is a rare combination. In our interviews with candidates, we were intentional about crafting questions that would help us discern whether the candidate was a theological fit as well as a cultural and competency fit.

Many search committees don't have a clear understanding of what their church's theological operating system is. While you may be at a "Presbyterian" church, your congregation likely has nuances that need to be fleshed out before simply accepting a "Presbyterian" candidate as a match. The same could be said for any denomination. The issue becomes even more nuanced among nondenominational churches (that now outnumber denominational churches in the US). Be sure you know what your church believes before beginning to look for a new leader or team member.

Because of the nuances of ministry, your committee must be intentional about the interview process, crafting it to your church's specific needs in a pastoral candidate.

Interviewing Candidates for Pastoral Attributes

There are many resources for assessing candidates in the corporate arena, but unfortunately, not many such resources exist for the church world. The metrics and desired qualities in pastoral candidates are much different than those that corporate candidates are measured against.

The pool of pastor search jokes is pretty thin, but here is a good reflection point on people we know well but who wouldn't make the cut for most modern-day Senior Pastor positions. The author of the following excerpt is unknown.

> **Adam:** Good man but problems with his wife. Also one reference told of how his wife and he enjoy walking nude in the woods.
>
> **Noah:** Former pastorate of 120 years with not even one convert. Prone to unrealistic building projects.

Abraham: Though the references reported wife-swapping, the facts seem to show he never slept with another man's wife, but did offer to share his own wife with another man.

Joseph: A big thinker, but a braggart, believes in dream-interpreting, and has a prison record.

Moses: A modest and meek man, but poor communicator, even stuttering at times. Sometimes blows his stack and acts rashly. Some say he left an earlier church over a murder charge.

David: The most promising leader of all until we discovered the affair he had with his neighbor's wife.

Solomon: Great preacher but our relocation costs for all his wives are out of our budget.

Elijah: Prone to depression. Collapses under pressure.

Elisha: Reported to have lived with a single widow while at his former church.

Hosea: A tender and loving pastor but our people could never handle his wife's occupation.

Jeremiah: Emotionally unstable, alarmist, negative, always lamenting things, reported to have taken a long trip to bury his underwear on the bank of a foreign river.

Isaiah: On the fringe? Claims to have seen angels in church. Has trouble with his language.

Jonah: Refused God's call into ministry until he was forced to obey by getting swallowed up by a great fish. He told us the fish later spit him out on the shore near here. We hung up.

Amos: Too backward and unpolished. With some seminary training he might have promise, but has a hang-up against wealthy people—might fit in better in a poor congregation.

Melchizedek: Great credentials at current work-place, but where does this guy come from? No information on his résumé about former work records. Every line about parents was left blank and he refused to supply a birth date.

John: Says he is a Baptist, but definitely doesn't dress like one. Has slept in the outdoors for months on end, has a weird diet, and provokes denominational leaders.

Peter: Too blue collar. Has a bad temper—even has been known to curse. Had a big run-in with Paul in Antioch. Aggressive, but a loose cannon.

Paul: Powerful CEO type leader and fascinating preacher. However, short on tact, unforgiving with younger ministers, harsh and has been known to preach all night.

James and John: Package deal preacher and associate seemed good at first, but found out they have an ego problem regarding other fellow workers and seating positions. Threatened an entire town after an insult. Also known to try to discourage workers who didn't follow along with them.

Timothy: Too young!

Methuselah: Too old . . . WAY too old!

Jesus: Has had popular times, but once His church grew to 5,000 He managed to offend them all, and then this church dwindled down to twelve people. Seldom stays in one place very long. And, of course, He's single.

Judas: His references are solid. A steady plodder. Conservative. Good connections. Knows how to

handle money. We're inviting him to preach this
Sunday. Possibilities here.

As we walk alongside churches in their Senior Pastor
searches, we've been asked time and time again for tools that
can help churches assess Senior Pastor candidates. Personality
tests, years of experience, reference and background checks,
and preaching samples should all be considered when assessing
a potential Lead Pastor. Even some of the corporate assessment
tools can be helpful to gain insight into the "CEO"-type qualities many churches desire of their Senior Pastor.

When you're down to your final candidates, how do you
dive deeper than outward-facing personality qualities to determine the intangible qualities that need to be assessed?

Let's look at the perfect example . . .

Jesus, the perfect shepherd.

The classic understanding of the facets of Christ's work is
that He was Prophet, Priest, and King. While we know that we
can't hire Jesus, I've found that assessing pastoral candidates in
these three facets is incredibly helpful. A good pastor should
reflect competencies in all three of these key areas.

Made more plain, the three components of an effective
Senior Pastor are preaching/teaching (prophet), leader/CEO
(king), and pastor (priest). To that end, I would give equal
weight to measuring all three of these areas. That means that
in addition to reviewing sermons and using assessment tools to
determine their leadership capacity, you should also examine
candidates' pastoral capacity.

These less tangible qualities of pastoral candidates fall under the umbrella of "shepherding" or "pastoring." To assess a candidate's pastoral gifts, I'd ask questions in the following three key areas:

1. Shepherd

Your next Senior Pastor must have connectivity to the congregation as a shepherd. Frankly, this is the ability of the candidate to be liked, and it is the biggest "must have" in a pastoral skill set. People will not learn from someone they do not like. The best preacher may not be the one whose teaching is best received. Unlike CEOs, or even politicians, a 50-percent approval rating (or "likability" rating) just won't cut it in a church.

How does the candidate talk about his current or previous congregation(s)? Does he relate to them as a shepherd? How does he see his role in their lives? How has the candidate shown emotional intelligence?

2. Bedside manner

How does the congregation feel about the pastor as he relates to them interpersonally?

Depending on the size of your church, the ideal candidate will not be able to be make hospital visit, but they must engender a spirit among the vast majority of the congregation that causes them to believe that their pastor cares very much about them.

Ask interview questions about previous pastoral care situations. Ask about particularly difficult pastoral dilemmas they have faced, or a particularly difficult funeral/tragedy that they have had to navigate. Ask how they have found ways to replicate or delegate their pastoral care in a thoughtful and prayerful way. The best answer is not simply "I hired a pastoral care person," but instead a much more thoughtful approach to pastoral care among their congregation. Seek to discern your pastoral candidate's heart for his congregation.

3. A CALLING TO REACH HURTING PEOPLE

This area isn't necessarily a barometer of their gift of mercy or sympathy because not all pastors will be high up on that range of qualities. However, in every pastor there needs to be more than a desire to preach and build an organization. There needs to be a deep-seated calling to minister to a broken world.

To assess this, I'd ask about the reasons they entered ministry. Ask them what they worry about when they go to bed at night. Ask them to give an example of a time or day in ministry when they went to bed thinking, "I did what I was called to do today." The answer should have something to do with helping people and not just preaching well or launching a fun new corporate initiative.

4. PRAYER

Jesus had a rich and profound prayer life, always connected to what God's will was for Him. A Senior Pastor without a rich prayer life is a Senior Pastor who is not seeking God's direction for your church, not filled up, and possibly on the verge of burnout.

Ask questions to determine the state of your candidates' prayer life. Ask them how they reconnect with Jesus and the Bible when they're feeling drained. Ask them how they seek God's direction, how God speaks to them, and how they seek God's will. Ask them what they do to "fill up" spiritually so that they are able to pour themselves into their role and their church.

This is just a sampling of intangible pastoral qualities and the questions to ask to assess those areas. I urge you not to overlook any one of the necessary facets of a Senior Pastor—their preaching and teaching (Prophet), their leadership capabilities (King), and their pastoral traits (Priest). Though the pastoral traits are more difficult to assess, they are vital to ensure that your next Senior Pastor is one who feeds and nurtures your congregation and guides your church into its next chapter.

Interviewing Candidates for Cultural Fit

When assessing a cultural fit between your church and the candidates you are interviewing, there are several factors to keep in mind. A cultural fit includes chemistry, competency, and theological fit. If one of those factors is missing, the candidate might not be a long-term fit and your search committee might find itself searching again.

Interviewing for Chemistry Fit

Every church is unique, which means every church staff is unique. The search team should have a proper understanding of their church staff's leadership structure and how they make decisions so that they can effectively interview for a chemistry fit.

When interviewing a candidate for chemistry, look for an alignment in vision and values. This stage in the interview process is why it is vital that your church have its mission, vision, and values written down to refer to when interviewing.

Some questions you may consider asking when interviewing for a chemistry fit are:

- Which of our church's values most resonate with you?
- How do you define the role of a pastor?
- How would you describe your leadership and team-building style?
- How do you manage conflict on a team?

Interviewing for Competency Fit

Competency is more difficult to interview for than one would think, especially in a ministry setting where the result is life change. This is the part of the interview process where an agreed-upon job description with key result areas is helpful. When there is not an agreed-upon document, search committees risk facing conflict because they are not on the same page regarding what they are interviewing for.

Some questions you may consider asking when interviewing for a competency fit are:

- What would your first ninety days look like in this role?
- Which of the key result areas is most exciting to you, and which is the most challenging?

- Tell us about a time when you achieved _____ in the key result area in a previous position.
- What do you think will be the most challenging part of this pastoral role?

Interviewing for Theological Fit

Theology is a vital component of a ministry position and one of the most intimidating factors for committee members to interview for. The first step in effectively interviewing for a theology match is to have a statement of faith document that the search committee understands and can explain. Smart candidates will ask the search committee for this during the interview process and will ask the committee questions regarding specific theological nuances.

Some questions you may consider asking when interviewing for a theological fit are:

- If you were to write a statement of faith for your personal ministry, what would it include?
- What most resonates with you about our statement of faith?
- What areas of theology have caused a source of conflict in your previous ministry roles?
- Describe your personal theology.
- Describe the pillars of biblical evangelical theology.

As we've discussed in every chapter of this book, the ultimate guide to the interviewing process is the spiritual discernment for which your pastor search committee must continually pray. As you pray about the one whom God is leading to your church, I hope these questions about pastoral attributes and cultural fit are helpful to your search committee.

Chapter 9

LANDING THE PLANE—THE HIRING PROCESS

You've voted on your final candidate. Now what?

Hiring a new pastor is always an exciting and somewhat scary time. There's a lot at stake, and it's critical to get it right. Once your church's search committee and decision makers decide on the candidate they want to hire, it's time to begin putting the offer together.

Communicate Regularly and Don't Move Too Slowly

It is vital that during this stage, just as in the interview process, you communicate openly with the candidate and not move too slowly. When you move slowly, you risk losing the candidate due to impatience or competing job offers. If you don't communicate well and often with the candidate during the interview process, they may begin to think that is indicative of the communication on your staff.

We often talk about the two hats that search teams need to wear when interviewing pastor candidates: the discernment hat ("Is this the right person for the job?") and the recruitment hat ("How do we effectively show them we think they're a great fit for the team?"). Churches sometimes lose great candidates simply because they focus so much on the discernment hat that they forget that the candidate has a choice to make as well. If the candidate doesn't feel wanted, they'll drop out of the process.

Be Transparent

Another mistake churches make happens when they've found the person they want to hire as their next Senior Pastor and they pull out all the stops to convince him to join their team.

Here's our perspective on this situation: As we interview candidates for our clients, we ask them why they left their previous church. Often, we hear about a church that presented themselves and the job in a way that they thought the candidate wanted to hear during the interviews, only for the candidate to find out later that the church and the expectations for the role were completely different.

If you want your hires to stick, you need to be completely transparent with your candidates from the very beginning. No church is perfect. Be honest with the candidate about the church's situation and the expectations of the role. What are the growth points for your church? What are the blind spots of your church or where things tend to fall flat? Have you provided a clear and accurate job description? Make sure to offer the candidate clear, measurable goals for success for the position.

One great way to be completely transparent with your pastor candidates is to give them references for your church. Churches always ask for references for the candidate, but what if the church provided some references of previous or current staff members who can talk to the candidate about what it's really like to work there? Give them names of people to connect with on staff to hear more about the heart of the church and team.

Complete Thorough Reference and Background Checks

If you haven't already, the church must complete background and reference checks on the candidate before making the job offer. One of the biggest mistakes you can make in your hiring process is skipping the background and reference checks on your potential new Senior Pastor. A reference check is your opportunity to protect your church and learn how your pastor candidate has led congregations and staffs in the past. Here are a few tips on conducting effective background checks.

Dig Deep

We have a list of questions we ask each reference that attempt to paint a broad picture of the candidate from work ethic to leadership abilities. It is also important to ask difficult questions that you may feel uncomfortable asking. For example, "Have you ever suspected the presence of an inappropriate relationship?" is a difficult question to ask but is an important one to protect both yourself and your ministry.

Ask Follow-up Questions

Conducting reference checks is a great opportunity to ask any remaining questions or to confirm the candidate's recall of events following your initial interview with the candidate. You may have further questions that your pastoral candidate was unable to answer, or perhaps the answers didn't satisfy you. Keep track of these questions and ask them to the references.

Use a Reliable Third-Party Company for Your Background checks

The background check is equally as important as the reference check, so be sure you use a reliable company that can conduct a criminal, credit, and education verification. Also, be sure you receive a signed release from the candidate giving you permission to conduct the background check. We conduct the entire reference, background, and credit check process for our clients to ensure they receive a 360-degree view of their potential hire.

Know What You Will Do with the Information Once You Have Completed the Checks

Information from your church background checks report should be made available to all decision makers and be a part of the final hiring decision. If the report comes back clear and positive, congratulations! You have a new hire. However, if there are questions that arise through the reference and background check, we suggest continuing conversations with the candidate in an effort to get clarity on your findings. Don't use a blanket determination to reject all candidates with a negative mark on their background check. We all have a story, and some of us may have an especially messy history before Christ entered our story.

A misconception about conducting church background checks is that they are intended to "dig up dirt" on a potential hire. This is not the case. The process of conducting church background checks is intended for you to get to know your potential new team member better and gain clarity on whether they would be a good fit for your team or not.

Making the Offer

I read a study a while back that claimed that most car wrecks happen within a mile of the destination. I don't know if that's true with cars, but I know it's true in pastoral searches. Most wrecks happen in the last part of the journey. Learning how to manage the compensation negotiations and final parts of the search can make all the difference between a great outcome and a disaster.

The first step in putting together the offer (in written form) for your potential new Senior Pastor is to determine the salary and benefits package you will be offering.

When your search committee put together your church profile and ideal Senior Pastor profile, you most likely settled on the salary range that you would be willing and able to pay your new Senior Pastor. Our team conducts comprehensive compensation consultations that help church boards and staffs know what to pay a new or existing team member, factoring cost of living, church size, church budget, and more.

Factors to keep in mind when determining the salary offer include: the candidate's salary history, how high-capacity and in demand they are, the market value for the position, your church's budget, the cost of living in your area, the salaries of the rest of your team, what benefits you are offering, and the candidate's family situation.

Don't underestimate how much it costs to move a family. Even the most inexpensive move will likely cost several thousands of dollars. We've found that churches don't always build this cost into their budget, and it can become a serious tension point in the onboarding process (or the candidate's decision to take the job or not). Not tangibly helping a new hire and his family with their move could lead to an early exit. It's important to make the new hire and his family members feel like you are taking care of them.

We have seen churches offer relocation assistance in amounts as small as $3,000 and as large as $50,000. We have also seen a church give a person a $100,000 zero-percent loan to purchase a house and then $20,000 of the loan is forgiven for each year so that in five years the pastor doesn't owe anything back to the church. This kind of bonus will depend on your church's financial ability and what you feel the Lord is calling you to do for your new pastor. Whatever you are able to offer, include the relocation stipend in your offer letter.

The next thing to include in your offer letter is your benefits package. Do you provide the housing (and/or pay the rent or a housing stipend) for your pastor? Do you offer health insurance? Disability and/or life insurance? A life insurance plan for your next pastor should, at bare minimum, be enough to cover all mortgages as well as all expenses and tuition for the family for a minimum of three years. Do you offer a 403(b) or 401(k) for your employees? What about a housing allowance? Do you provide an HSA or HRA plan? Can you offer health club/gym memberships? Do you provide childcare stipends? Do you offer a cell phone or transportation stipend?

Also include in the offer letter anything you provide as far as professional development and sabbaticals. Do you provide an amount for conferences, training, and whatever else could keep your pastor renewed? Do you include any kind of financial training or counseling opportunities for your pastor and his family? Include all of these in your offer letter.

Salary Negotiations

I do not know a seminary that teaches pastors how to negotiate salaries. They are woefully ill equipped and tend to make mistakes that have potential to hinder their family's financial needs, both in the short term and the long term. I have seen many committees make mistakes in the salary negotiation phase of the search and encounter immense frustration that often leads them back to ground zero in their pastoral search. Most often, the tension points in the salary negotiation phase are over a small amount of money.

Here are a few tips for you as you negotiate salary:

1. Give a signing bonus, not an annual increase

This is typically an effective solution when there is dis-agreement in the salary. Offering a signing bonus can help reduce anxiety for the new pastor, especially if he must move his family from another state. It allows them to feel comfort-able making a change while minimizing financial risk for the church. It gives the opportunity for the pastor to set and achieve engagement, discipleship, and growth goals with the potential of a raise or bonus structure upon meeting those goals.

2. Spend a little more, because restarting the search is more expensive

One of the biggest mistakes we see search committees make is not accounting for the immense amount of time and loss of momentum accumulated during the search process. We've seen committees restart the entire pastor search process again after a disagreement over a few thousand dollars. Before making a rash decision, be sure the entire search committee thinks through a cost-benefit analysis of giving a signing bonus versus restarting the entire search process.

3. Don't be held hostage by someone who "needs more money"

If you have compromised with the candidate and done your best to set the candidate up for financial success but they are still asking for more money, be cautious. While you shouldn't let a small amount of money cause an unraveling in the search process, you should also avoid being held hostage by someone who always seems to "need more money." This should raise questions about the ability of the candidate to live within his or her means and overall financial stewardship. The way a candidate handles his finances is a pretty good indicator of how he will handle the church's. Avoid this by asking the candidate for his financial expectations early in the process and not waiting until the end when you're ready to make an offer.

4. INSIST ON A CREDIT CHECK, AND DON'T HIRE PEOPLE DEEP IN DEBT

Unfortunately, many pastors find themselves in more debt than they can handle. Be sure the search committee conducts a thorough credit check on the candidate before making an offer. With people who are over their head in debt, you'll never be able to pay them enough. This is a key step in assessing the financial stewardship capacity of the candidate you are considering.

Consider a Social Contract

When you hire a new employee, there's usually a stack of paperwork to sign: typical federal forms, organizational codes of conduct, organizational manuals, and procedure standards. Has your church or organization ever considered developing and implementing a social contract?

So, what is a social contract? In short, it's an agreement employees make with each other on how to communicate and interact with one another. The people on your ministry team will communicate (let's hope—otherwise, maybe we need to take a step back!), so why not ensure that everyone has the same expectations? This can reach beyond paid church staff and influence volunteers or even committed church members. It builds trust and communicates a desire to have a positive environment where dialogue is welcome.

In developing your social contract, it's important for you to get feedback from the people it affects, namely, the members of your ministry team. If this seems like a daunting task due to the size of your organization, ask your managers to gather what works and what doesn't from their individual teams. Having everyone's perspective, regardless of their position, is key to ensuring the social contract works effectively across the board.

Accountability is built into the social contract. Everyone from the head of an organization to the volunteers must believe in it or it won't work. When everyone on the ministry team knows what's accepted and encouraged and what isn't, it allows freedom for anyone to chip in if someone isn't acting in accordance. If your social contract calls for positive talk and keeping negative, pessimistic commentary aside, situations when this occurs can be dealt with objectively.

As your organization grows or changes, it's important to measure how your social contract is working and adjust it. It's also important to communicate to your ministry team that a social contract isn't a behavioral modification document but instead a valuable tool in ensuring everyone on your team really is on the same team.

Introducing Your New Senior Pastor

You've gotten through the potentially stressful pastor search process, found a candidate who is a great fit, extended an offer, and successfully hired a new Senior Pastor. All of your work is over, right?

Well, not quite. Once the offer is accepted, part of "landing the plane" is introducing your new pastor to your church staff, congregation, and community. This is an exciting time for both your new pastor and your church body, and it's also a pretty important one. How a Senior Pastor—and the entire family—is introduced and welcomed to your church sets the tone for their time there.

Here are five tips for how to introduce your new Senior Pastor to your church team, congregation, and the surrounding community.

1. Assign a Point Person

It's easy for any introduction events to be overlooked if there isn't someone specifically responsible for making sure they happen. Be sure to appoint one person to oversee all of the introduction activities. One of the most obvious choices for this person is your pastor search committee chairperson or the person on your church staff in charge of communications and/ or events.

2. Spread the Big Announcement

Ideally, you have communicated well with the church staff and the congregation throughout the pastor search process.

The introduction announcement is your final piece of communication. If, throughout the process, your primary means of communicating has been through church-wide e-mail, then your first step is to e-mail the church body to announce that the new leader has been hired. If your primary means of communication has been through announcements, slides, or a church bulletin, then use those.

If you haven't already done so during the final interview process, include pictures and information about the new pastor and his family so that your congregation can begin to get to know him. Where are they from? Where did they go to school? How long have they been married? What ages are the children? Where has the pastor served previously? What are some of their hobbies? Also include why the new Senior Pastor is excited to become their new leader.

One great way to do this, if you have the capacity, is to create an introduction video with your new leader and his family. That way your pastor can introduce himself and his family and say why they are looking forward to joining your church team. Have fun with this!

3. Hold a Commissioning or Welcoming Service

Some churches have a commissioning service or special welcoming service to announce their new pastor. It's a time to praise God for the one whom He has brought to your church, prayerfully seek His direction for the next season of ministry, and hear your new leader preach his first sermon as your Senior Pastor.

Throughout the introduction process, it's vitally important that the spouse and family also feel very welcome. Taking a new job, moving, and switching churches and schools can take quite an emotional toll on a family, and they may not feel all of the "welcoming" that your new pastor feels in his limelight. Go out of your way to make his spouse and children feel included, cared for, and welcome.

4. Host a Special Staff Dinner or Two or Ten

Though your new Senior Pastor will be leading an entire church body, they will be leading and interacting with the church staff more directly. Make sure you host an event—or several—that gives your new pastor the chance to get to know their new team. This can be done in large and/or small group settings.

It might be a good idea to ask your new leader for his input on how they would prefer to get to know everyone. For example, when Tim Stevens joined our team, he took the entire team out to lunch—two staff members at a time—over the course of a couple of months. Tim intentionally got to know us all in smaller group settings over meals. Make sure you facilitate this kind of onboarding with your new pastor.

5. Get Social

Once the new Senior Pastor has been introduced to the church staff and congregation, it's time to get the word out to your community. Announce your new pastor on your website, on all of your social media accounts, in a press release to your local newspaper, and/or in an interview on your local faith-based radio station.

Again, be sure to include visual elements like pictures and videos as much as possible. Getting the word out there may even attract more visitors to your church.

As you plan special dinners, services, receptions, videos, etc., for your new leader and his family, be sure to inform all involved of the plans, and schedule everything ahead of time so that the family can prepare accordingly.

Welcoming Your New Senior Pastor

The offer has been made and accepted. The new pastor is set to move to your city next week. Your job is finished until he walks through the door and you hand him the Church Staff Employee Handbook, right?

If you've ever moved your family to a new city to start a new job, you know how overwhelming it can feel. From finding a new home to enrolling the kids in school, there is a long list of things that can be stressful for the new pastor's family. Here are some ways you can celebrate and greet your new pastor to ensure they feel loved and welcome in their new church community.

Before your new pastor arrives, send the family these suggestions so they can best plan their moving day/weekend:

- Map (or links) to local necessities—Target, Walgreens, grocery, etc.
- Recommended doctors and pediatricians
- Local emergency numbers—hospitals, poison control, etc.

- Trusted service providers—auto mechanic, cleaning service, etc.
- Professionals who are church members—dentists, doctors, hairstylists, personal trainers, lawyers, etc.
- Trusted realtors or advice on neighborhoods if housing is not provided
- Suggested date night locations and trusted sitters

Use your committee as a resource for the above lists. There is probably already a wealth of answers within your church body.

When the candidate arrives at his new home, here are a few suggested items to bring by on moving day:

- A box of household goods for the family to open when they arrive at their new home: toilet paper, paper towels, hand soap, cleaning supplies, some snacks for while they unpack, a gift certificate to a local pizza place, etc.
- A gift or gift basket for the family: age-appropriate toys for kids, a book about the area, an appliance such as a new stove, dishwasher, or laundry machines, a welcome sign from the church, etc.
- A hot meal or two for the family

Onboarding Your New Senior Pastor

First days are hard, even if the new pastor is high capacity and ready to get started. The amount of information a new pastor is expected to learn can be equated to the old saying,

"It's like drinking out of a fire hose." Everything is new—new names, new programs, new responsibilities, and new office norms. There are many things that the search committee can do to make the onboarding process more productive for your new pastor.

Communicate with Your New Pastor before Their Arrival

After the offer is signed, communicate with him about moving assistance, their start date, and what the first few days on the job will look like. As we mentioned above, if your new pastor is moving to a new area to join your church's staff, go the extra mile and prepare for the arrival at his new house. A "welcome kit" with essentials for the new home will go a long way in making your new staff member feel loved. Before they walk through the doors on the first day, make sure you've shared with your new pastor all the names and faces he needs to know.

Ensure Everything Is Set Up before Their Arrival

There is nothing worse for a new pastor than showing up for the first day of work and feeling like the church was unprepared for his arrival. Make sure his office is set up, clean, and in good working order. Call IT to establish user IDs for his login and e-mail. Ensure his computer is new or at the very least wiped clear of the previous owner's materials and ready for them. Label office keys and give them to the new pastor on a key ring (don't just hand them random keys). In short, show him that you are excited about him joining your church by preparing for the arrival.

Give Them a Copy of the Employee Handbook and/or Social Contract

If your church doesn't have an Employee Handbook, write one. If the employee handbook is out of date, update it. An Employee Handbook should include as much information about the organization as possible including your church's story, vision, values, and practices as well as Human Resource information on health and dental insurance, retirement plans, and paid time off. A section on behavior and work expectations would also be beneficial. If you have a social contract, as we explained earlier, make sure he has a copy. An Employee Handbook and/or social contract says to your new pastor, "We care enough about you to communicate what you can expect from us and what we expect of you."

Set Up a Schedule for Them for Their First Few Days and Weeks

Set up meetings for your new pastor with other church staff members, board members, and key lay leaders/volunteer leaders. By giving structure to their first few days, you will allow them to meet people and get acquainted with their new role.

Tell your new pastor the point people for different types of questions. Your new pastor should know the people within the church who can help them become acclimated to your church's culture. Every church is different; even if the pastor fits your church's culture to a T, he will still have questions about norms and expectations. Make sure you have people assigned to help the pastor's family get plugged into the church and the surrounding neighborhoods.

Have an Onboarding Plan Not Only for Your New Pastor but Also for Their Family

Think of ways to connect your pastor's family in the community during their first few weeks there. Take the family out to lunch to celebrate their first day. Have staff members bring over dinners for the first week to both ease with the moving stress and begin to form friendships. Provide them with a guide to nearby restaurants, shopping centers, schools, and anything else that may be of interest to their family.

Give the pastor's spouse a place to "go" that onboards them into the community. Remember, your new staff member has built-in opportunities on the job to connect with people in the church, but the wife may find herself alone and isolated. Have the head of your women's ministry reach out and invite her to something. It's important that the entire family, not just the candidate, feel warmly welcomed by your community. This will go a long way in retaining your new pastor and making the entire family feel welcome.

Give Them Time to Grow Into Their Role and Flourish

Getting your new staff member on board quickly is a great goal, and most of our clients tell us that they want someone who can "hit the ground running" and "plug and play from day one." That's completely understandable, but it's not always realistic.

While your new pastor might have all the skills and experiences you need and may match your culture and DNA perfectly, he still has to acclimate to his surroundings and get

to know how you operate. He comes into your culture without any firsthand knowledge of the key lay leaders they'll need to connect with and mobilize to be effective. He will have to get to know your organizational personality and learn how decisions get made and implemented. Also, he will likely have a family that he need to pay attention to as they get acclimated to the new surroundings. All of that will take time. Most of your new hires won't be effective and running at full speed until at least six months into the new position and sometimes longer than that.

If you want to hold on to your new pastor, be patient with them. All of the steps listed above can shorten the time it takes to get him to the place where he is effective in ministry and enjoying the process. But patience is key to allow him to grow, flourish, and be the leader your church needs.

Signing the contract is not the final step in hiring a new pastor. A well-planned and thoughtful welcoming and onboarding process is the best way to get a new pastor to love his new role and jump into leading your congregation and church staff. You owe it to your new pastor—and to your congregation and staff—to onboard them and his family well.

Chapter 10

CONCLUSION

I started Vanderbloemen Search Group six years ago because I had firsthand experience of the challenges of being under-resourced in church staffing as both a lay leader and a Senior Pastor in the church. I graduated seminary as a bright-eyed young leader ready to win the world for Jesus. I quickly realized that even with a Princeton Seminary degree, I was not equipped with practical resources concerning leading a church staff and board through the pastor search process. These nine chapters come from my team's experience consulting with more than seven hundred pastor search teams all over the country through the beautifully complex pastor search process. I speak for myself and my team when I say that leaders in the church like you who are passionate about furthering the kingdom by equipping your church with resources like this keep us going each day.

The pastor search process requires relentless emotional, spiritual, and physical energy and is not for the weak. It is an immense responsibility to serve the Bride of Christ through a prayerful pastor search process that should not be taken lightly. It requires a special group of people who are in tune with what God has called them to as a church.

It is my prayer that through this handbook, you have learned:

- Scripture verses for prayer and guidance as your search committee seeks your new pastor
- How to communicate and grieve the loss of a Senior Pastor
- Practical steps to forming your church's pastor search committee
- The time line and expectations of the pastor search process
- The importance of knowing your church's mission, vision, values, and culture
- How to find potential pastoral candidates
- How to vet and interview potential pastoral candidates
- How to properly hire and onboard your new pastor

Even after nine chapters of practical tips and resources, I cannot stress enough the importance of prayer and spiritual discernment through your church's pastor search process. There is no cookie-cutter process or magic formula that will help you find the right fit for your church.

Our team at Vanderbloemen Search Group would be honored to be a resource to you and your pastor search committee as you discern whom God is leading to your church. We specialize in pastoral search, succession planning, staff consultation, and compensation analysis consultations.

E-mail me at info@vanderbloemen.com or call me at 713-300-9665.

Thank you for your investment in the life of your church. I look forward to joining you as we build the kingdom here on earth.

Sincerely,

William Vanderbloemen

Appendix A

PASTOR SEARCH COMMITTEE PRAYER CALENDAR

Six-Month Congregational Pastor Search Prayer Calendar

The pastor search process can be a stressful and anxiety-filled chapter in a church's history. Our team has created this prayer calendar to help you and your church pray through this crucial time in your church's life. While your church's pastor search process is unique, we hope this prayer calendar acts as a guide to help you know how to pray for your church leaders and congregation during this exciting time.

Month 1: True Needs of the Congregation

This month, your pastor search committee will be creating a time line and a pastoral profile for your church's ideal candidates based on the church's ministry needs, vision, mission, and values.

Pray that the true needs of the congregation will come to the surface as the church staff and committee seek the Lord about what is next for your church. Pray that no personal agenda would surface but only the will of the Lord as the pastor search committee and staff seek what He has next for the congregation.

> And God placed all things under his feet and appointed him to be head over everything for the church, which is his body, the fullness of him who fills everything in every way. (Eph. 1:22–23)

Month 2: Clarity on Pastoral Job Description

This month, your pastor search committee will be writing the job description for the pastor profile based on the needs of your church.

Pray that the pastor search committee will have clarity as to the characteristics, goals, and key result areas that should be included in the job description for the church's next pastor. Pray that the committee would not settle for too little or aim too high, making the job description unreasonable or unattainable. Pray that the committee would agree upon the background and experience needed in the next pastor.

> The saying is trustworthy: If anyone aspires to the office of overseer, he desires a noble task. Therefore an overseer must be above reproach. (1 Tim. 3:1–2 ESV)

Month 3: Hearing God's Voice

This month, your pastor search committee will begin receiving and evaluating applications from candidates.

Pray that the committee would hear God's voice with clarity and feel peace as they discern whom they should interview. Pray that as they read applications, listen to sermon samples, and talk with candidates, they place the church's needs and desires before their own.

> "I am the good shepherd; I know my sheep and my sheep know me." (John 10:14)

Month 4: Asking the Right Questions

This month, your pastor search committee will begin interviewing candidates with the most promise to be your next pastor.

Pray that the pastor search committee will know the right questions to ask as they represent the church through the interview process. Pray that they would represent the church accurately and attractively. Pray that they would have clarity as they interview candidates, eliminate candidates, and move forward with candidates throughout the interview process.

> In the same way, let your light shine before others, so that they may see your good works and give glory to your Father who is in heaven. (Matt. 5:16 ESV)

Month 5: Peace for Future Pastor's Family

This month, the pastor search committee has likely narrowed the pool of candidates down to a few finalists and is praying over whom God has called to lead your church. This might mean that the committee has a finalist who is currently in view of a call.

Pray that the future pastor, the spouse, and family would feel the same peace and excitement that the pastor search committee feels about the candidate. Pray that the candidate and their family will have clarity during their visits with the church and know whether or not this is the next step in ministry to which God has called them.

> And the peace of God, which passeth all understanding, shall keep your hearts and minds through Christ Jesus. (Phil. 4:7 KJV)

Month 6: Peace for the Congregation

This month, the pastor search committee will likely be submitting an offer to your church's next pastor.

Pray that the entire congregation would feel a sense of peace and confirmation as the pastor is confirmed through congregational meetings and/or a congregational voting process. Pray that there is unity among the search committee, church staff, and congregation. Pray that no one person would have an agenda that would cause a distraction or deterrent from God's work throughout the pastor search process. Pray that the new pastor and their family have a smooth transition into their new church and community.

> Above all, clothe yourselves with love, which ties everything together in unity. (Col. 3:14 ISV)

Appendix B

SAMPLE PASTOR SEARCH COMMITTEE MEMBER AGREEMENT

Electing members to your pastor search committee is an extremely important decision for any church. Your pastor search committee will shape the future of your church and its kingdom impact as they seek the next pastor God is calling to lead your congregation.

Because serving on a pastor search committee is such a significant contribution to the future of your church, it's necessary that the members be completely dedicated to their role on the committee. Their earnest commitment to prayerfully and steadfastly seeking the best candidate for your church staff is vital.

Many pastor search committees require their members to sign an agreement or a "covenant" that fleshes out the specifics of their commitment. It can be difficult to discern everything that should be included in such an agreement.

Feel free to use and customize the Pastor Search Committee Member Agreement template.

Pastor Search Committee Member Agreement

I, _____, a member of the Pastor Search Committee of _____ Church, agree wholeheartedly to serve the committee and my church by prayerfully seeking the next _____ that God is calling to lead our congregation. Along with my fellow Pastor Search Committee members and relying on the guidance of the Holy Spirit, I commit to the following (please initial):

_____ We will pray earnestly and seek God's direction in this hire.

_____ We will agree on clear roles and responsibilities for the committee members.

_____ We will set a goal time line for the search process and strive to stay on task.

_____ We will set a meeting schedule for our committee and hold to that schedule.

_____ We will decide on how our final agreement and hire is to be made, be it unanimous, consensus, majority, etc.

_____ As needed, we will seek input from the church staff and congregation as we develop the qualifications and traits desired in this hire.

_____ We will create a clear job description for our ideal candidate, striving for high but realistic standards.

_____ We will examine our hearts and seek the best candidate for this hire, free of any individual agendas.

_____ We will be intentional, thoughtful, consistent, and honest in our communication with the congregation, the church staff, the candidates, and each other.

_____ We will uphold the highest levels of respect and confidentiality, and we will clearly define what is to be kept confidential.

_____ We will agree to a vetting and interviewing process and stick to it, putting all final candidates through the same process.

_____ We will not delay in our communication with candidates.

_____ We will conduct background and reference checks of our final candidate(s) with all due diligence, notifying our candidate(s) if/when we are conducting said checks and upholding the confidentiality of our candidate(s).

_____ We will clearly and honestly present to our final candidates: our church's history, mission, vision, current financial situation, decision-making processes, team dynamics, organizational structure, limitations, challenges, and plans for our future.

_____ We will strive for peace, cooperation, respect, and unity in our discussions and decisions, eschewing conflict and, if it occurs, addressing it with prayer, humility, and love.

_____ We will hold one another accountable to this agreement, speaking the truth in love.

_____   _____

Name (please print)   Date

_____

Signature

Appendix C

SAMPLE PASTOR SEARCH COMMITTEE RETREAT AGENDA

Scheduling a pastor search committee retreat at the beginning of the process is an effective way to focus on the task at hand. By getting away and focusing all of the group's combined attention and brainpower, the search committee will become a more effective and aligned team. Make sure there is someone delegated to take and distribute notes of all that is discussed.

The following is an example of the search committee retreat agenda for a one-day retreat.

8:00–8:30 a.m.	Gather. Hand out and go over retreat agenda, purpose, and desired outcomes.
8:30–9:30 a.m.	Breakfast and prayer as a team.

9:30–11:15 a.m.	Delegate roles and responsibilities on the committee.
	Determine the committee's purpose and mission statement.
	Discuss the church's decision-making process.
	Determine the committee's decision-making process.
11:15–11:30 a.m.	Break
11:30–1:15 p.m.	Establish the search committee's meeting schedule.
	Determine ideal succession/Senior Pastor search time line.
	Conduct initial brainstorm session of places and ways to search.
1:15–2:15 p.m.	Lunch and prayer as a team
2:15–3:15 p.m.	Brainstorm: create church profile
3:15–4:00 p.m.	Break: team-building game or exercises
4:00–5:30 p.m.	Brainstorm: create ideal Pastor Profile/Job Description
5:30–6:30 p.m.	Address any questions, concerns, thoughts, and upcoming tasks. Assign any action items.
6:30–8:00 p.m.	Dinner and prayer as a team

Appendix D

SAMPLE PASTOR SEARCH COMMITTEE MEETING AGENDA

1. Prayer (5 minutes)

2. Big Picture Update (5–10 minutes)
   What has happened since the last meeting? Where are you in the process? Any additional updates?

3. Main Objective (15–30 minutes)
   What do you need to get accomplished during this meeting? Assigning roles and responsibilities? Assessing résumés of selected candidates?

4. Brainstorming Session
   Whom can you contact in your personal and professional networks? Where else can you search? Who might know someone qualified?

5. Next Steps and Action Items (10–15 minutes)

What is the next thing your committee needs to accomplish? Who is responsible for what? Assign the action items and deadlines.

6. Closing Prayer (5 minutes)

REFERENCE CHECK AUTHORIZATION FORM

Suggested e-mail to candidate:

Dear NAME,

CHURCH is beginning the Background, Credit, Education, and Reference Checks for your candidacy. I will be e-mailing you a Waiver Form to complete. If you could complete the form and return it as soon as possible, I would appreciate it.

For your reference check, we need the names, e-mail addresses, and phone numbers of five to six references. At least one (preferably two) of these references should be someone to whom you reported, one should be a colleague in a working relationship with you, and another should be one who reported to you (even a volunteer is fine). The remaining references can be anyone who knows you well. We prefer that none of the references be related to you.

If you have any questions, we would be happy to answer them.

Thank you,

SIGNATURE

Authorization form to send to candidate:

CRIMINAL, CREDIT, EDUCATION AND MORAL BACKGROUND CHECK AUTHORIZATION FORM

Full Name _____

Address _____

City/State/Zip _____

Home Phone _____

Social Security Number _____

Driver's License Number and State of Issuance _____

Date of Birth _____

Education Verification (List institutions, locations, degrees received, and completion dates) _____

_____

Position Being Considered For _____

By initialing below, I acknowledge that I have not failed to disclose any information that might be considered pertinent to the process for the hire of the above-mentioned position. This applies to any legal, moral, or ethical indiscretions. I also acknowledge that consideration for the above-mentioned position hinges on my legal (criminal and civil), financial, moral, ethical, and reputational background; as well as any past indiscretions and accusations, whether legal (criminal and civil), financial, moral, or ethical in nature.

_____

(Initial here)

PLEASE READ CAREFULLY

I hereby authorize the release of a consumer report for employment purposes to CHURCH. I understand that inquiry may include, but is not limited to: my credit history, education history, criminal arrest and conviction history, motor vehicle record, credit check, references, drug test results, and copies of prior personnel files through any investigative, credit agencies or bureaus of the choice of CHURCH. I also authorize the release of medical information as part of the consumer report for employment purposes.

_____

_____

(Candidate Signature)

Appendix F

SAMPLE REFERENCE CHECK FORMAT

Below are the topics to cover in your reference check. Be sure to document the conversation in an organized fashion so that the entire search committee can read through the conversation.

- Relationship of the reference to the candidate
- Description of candidate's personality
- Opinion of candidate's work quality
- Description of candidate's leadership style and gifting
- Candidate's ability to cast vision
- Candidate's ability to build and lead a team
- Opinion of candidate's marital relationship
- Candidate's strengths and weaknesses
- Candidate's teaching/preaching style
- Description of candidate's spiritual walk

These topics are simply a starting point for questions to ask the candidate's references. Be sure to tailor your questions to your church's specific needs.

Appendix G

LISTENING GUIDE FOR EVALUATING TEACHING/SERMON SAMPLES

Below is a listening guide to aid your search committee members as you evaluate teaching/sermon samples of your Senior Pastor candidates.

There are twelve questions for the areas of both presentation and content. Most of the questions are "yes" or "no" questions with space for additional comments. With many of the questions, answering "no" is not a count against them as a speaker; it merely helps to assess their style of teaching.

Use this to evaluate which candidates have the style and teaching that is the best fit for your congregation and your church's mission.

Presentation

1. Are they comfortable and confident? Yes No

_____

2. Do they pray before they begin? Yes No

_____

3. Do they capture your attention in the first thirty seconds?
Yes No

_____

4. Is their manner or speaking more: Casual Formal

_____

5. Are they well-spoken? Articulate? Yes No

_____

6. Do they have a good stage presence? Is it appropriate for the
venue in which they are speaking? Yes No

_____

7. Is it easy to follow him? Yes No

_____

8. Are they engaging? Easy to listen to? Yes No

_____

9. Was the sermon: Too Short   Too Long   Just Right

_____

10. Do they seem well prepared? Yes No

_____

11. Do they use their sense of humor? Yes No

_____

12. Is their passion for God's Word and His people evident?
Yes No

_____

Content

1. Do they go straight to Scripture? Yes No

_____

2. Is their style of teaching more: Exegetical Expositional Topical Textual Narrative

_____

3. Do they employ a: Freer Use of Text   Stricter Use of Text

_____

4. Do they appeal more to: The Heart   The Mind

_____

5. Do their illustrations boost your understanding of the Scripture/topic? Yes No

_____

6. Is the sermon well structured? Yes No

_____

7. Do you see evidence of originality in their teaching? Yes No

_____

8. How do they treat the text?

_____

9. Do they make the sermon practical/applicable? Yes No

_____

10. Is there evidence of great wisdom/insight? Yes No

_____

11. Is the message more: Encouraging Challenging Good Mix

_____

12. Is there a call to action at the end of the sermon? Yes No

_____

Appendix H

LIST OF PERSONALITY ASSESSMENTS

There are many personality assessments on the market that can help your search committee assess the strengths and weaknesses of your Senior Pastor candidates. Personality assessments should be looked at within the context of the whole person and not to put people in a box. People's personalities and leadership strengths shift and change over time, so be sensitive to the context of the profile as you review it.

We also recommend entire church staffs use these personality assessments to enhance communication, relationship building, and productivity among the team.

Below are a few of the most common assessments.

Insights Discovery Personal Profile

This profile is intended to help your search committee understand their working style and its impact on others. This profile covers the individual's conscious and less conscious states of interpersonal skills and communication styles. For more information, visit www.insights.com.

Leading from Your Strengths

This profile is designed specifically for those in ministry positions, as the language is pastoral and ministry focused. It reveals the individual's habitual patterns of behavior, thought, emotion, and communication. For more information, visit www.ministryinsights.com.

Myers-Briggs Type Indicator

This profile uses C. G. Jung's theory that people's seemingly random variation in behavior is actually quite orderly and consistent, due to the differences in the ways individuals prefer to use their perception and judgment. It specifically looks at the way the person views the world, assesses information, makes decisions, and views structure. For more information, visit www.myersbriggs.org.

DiSC

This profile is a personal assessment tool used to increase productivity, teamwork, and communication. It helps people better understand themselves and how to adapt their behaviors with others. For more information, visit www.discprofile.com.

Birkman Method

This profile integrates behavioral, motivational, and occupational data to predict behavior and work satisfaction across situations. It can help people improve people skills and align roles with relationships. For more information, visit www.birkman.com.

Appendix I

SAMPLE SENIOR PASTOR PROFILE/ JOB DESCRIPTION

As you write your job description, be sure you include information about the following:

Background and Skills

- **Education**—What level of educational experience are you comfortable with or requiring from candidates interested in this position? It is vital that your search committee is on the same page regarding what is required and what is preferred regarding education.
- **Experience**—Similar to education, what kind of experiences and skills do you want this person to have? Be sure that you know the difference between what is required and what is preferred.

- **Leadership**—What kind of leader do you want your Senior Pastor to be? What kind of leader will be best for your team?
- **Pastoral Style**—What kind of pastoral style is best for your church? Do you need a relational pastor or more of an operational pastoral style?
- **Communication**—What kind of preaching and teaching style are you looking for in your pastor? What does their communication style need to be in the day-to-day office?

Personal Characteristics to Consider

- Theology
- Spiritual Discipline
- Marriage Health
- Creativity
- Personality/Charisma
- Character
- Compassion
- Sense of Humor
- Visionary
- Collaborative
- Humility
- Heart of a Servant
- Lifelong Learner
- Builder
- Actionary

Appendix J

SAMPLE CHURCH PROFILE

Use these starting points to inspire your search committee as you create your church profile to share with candidates you are considering for the Senior Pastor role.

Church Operational Details

Budget for prior year and current year
Weekly attendance for prior year and current year
Staff head count for prior year and current year

Organization

Tell the story of the church. Who are you, where is your church from, who is your current pastor? What are your strategic plans for the future, and what are ways you plan to get there?

Vision, Mission, Values, Beliefs

What is the vision of your church? What do you hope to accomplish in the future? What are your core beliefs? What do you highly value?

Ministries

What different ministries does your church offer? What are you known for? What makes you unique? What do you do well? What keeps people coming back? Are you involved in the community? How can your members get involved in your church?

Weekends

When does your church meet? Do you have multiple service times? What style of service is it? How long do you meet? Is there more than one meeting location or campus? What do most people wear on a typical Sunday? Describe the worship and teaching styles.

Community

How does your community view your church? What is it like to live there? What makes your community unique?

Appendix K

SAMPLE ON-SITE INTERVIEW FORMAT

Example Schedule for First-Round On-Site Interviews

- **Noon arrival into airport, pickup**—We suggest that someone from the church/ministry be the person to drive the semifinalist around, and that they park and meet the candidate in the airport where passengers are exiting security and heading toward baggage. Personally greeting a candidate goes a long way toward a great first impression and making them feel welcome.
- **Late lunch**—While you may not be meeting as a full search team until the evening, we encourage you to invite the search team (and nobody else) to an informal lunch with the candidate. It's important that the candidate meets the committee and spends time with them. It's equally important that the staff not be

perceived as having an inordinate amount of time with the candidate.

- **Afternoon**—Plan a tour of your facilities and time for the candidate to meet and hang out with the senior staff. Drive around the city a bit. Don't spend too much time doing this, as you don't want to wear the candidate out before the interview. Use this time to get to know the candidate for who they are in a relaxed setting.

- **Rest and regroup time**—The candidate will want to call home and debrief with their family or prayer partners, mentors, etc. They will also have traveled all day and need a break. Drop them off at their hotel with a couple of hours to spare before your dinner/evening interview. We suggest the hotel you book for them has Wi-Fi, and you also might consider preparing a gift basket with snacks and something branded from the church/ministry, leaving it in their hotel room ahead of time as a nice surprise. You'd be surprised at how far this inexpensive gesture goes in making a great impression.

- **Dinner/Interview**—While restaurants are nice, homes are even better. If you have someone who can host a dinner in their home, it will give you all time together in an informal setting with the privacy and quiet you'll want for an interview. If not, perhaps you can get a private room within a restaurant.

- **Breakfast**—Arrange for an informal breakfast with whoever would like to join.

- **Airport for a noon departure**—Remember that it can take longer than you think to get through security. Drop the candidate off at the airport no later than ninety minutes before departure. Building in good time margins and staying on top of your schedule will send a positive message about working with you. Make sure the candidate knows whom they can contact with any questions.

Appendix L

SAMPLE SENIOR PASTOR
INTERVIEW QUESTIONS

1. Why are you looking for a new job?

2. What are your two greatest weaknesses?

3. How do you cope with stress?

4. What are your short-term and long-term goals?

5. Tell me about a time when you have both successfully and unsuccessfully handled conflict.

6. How do you develop team members and volunteers?

7. What constructive criticism have you received in the past that surprised you the most?

8. Describe the cultures of your last few job or church settings, how they differed, and which one fit you best.

9. Tell me about a time when you had to get people with different viewpoints to the same level of understanding.

10. How do you stay organized?

11. What most resonates with you about the opportunity to serve as the Senior Pastor of our church?

Appendix M

SAMPLE SUCCESSION/SENIOR PASTOR SEARCH TIME LINE

The following is an example of a Succession/Senior Pastor search time line using a twelve-month succession plan.

Time Remaining Until Succession	Action
11–12 months	• Elect the search committee members
	• Determine how the search committee will make decisions and how often they will meet
	• Designate roles on the search committee
	• Create the ideal Senior Pastor candidate profile

11–12 months *(continued)*	• Create the profile for your church
	• Research and decide whether or not you will hire a search firm to conduct your Senior Pastor search
10–11 months	• Develop a communication/prayer plan for the congregation throughout the search process
	• Announce the succession plan and search process according to the communication plan
	• If not hiring a search firm, develop a search process plan
	• Finalize the job description
	• Conduct a compensation analysis or hire a firm to conduct one for the Senior Pastor role to determine a fair and competitive salary to attract the desired candidates
6–9 months	• Officially launch the search for the next Senior Pastor
	• Begin advertising the role through appropriate channels, such as denominational media, seminaries, and job boards
	• Begin consistent meetings with the pastor search committee

3–5 months	• Begin sourcing, screening, and interviewing candidates according to the process previously established
2 months	• Determine your final slate of candidates and present to the church's decision makers
1 month	• Semi-finalists interview at your church
2 weeks	• Finalist(s) return with spouse(s) for broader interviews with more members of the leadership of the church
1 week	• Offer extended and accepted

ABOUT THE AUTHOR

William Vanderbloemen (MDiv, Princeton Theological Seminary) is the president and CEO of Vanderbloemen Search Group, the leading search firm specifically focused on connecting churches and ministries with the right leadership for their teams.

William has been able to combine his ministry experience as a Senior Pastor with the best practices of executive search to provide churches with a unique offering: a deep understanding of local church work with the very best knowledge and practices of professional executive search.

William studied executive search under a mentor with more than twenty-five years of executive search at the highest level. He learned the best corporate practices, including the search strategies used by the internationally known firm Russell Reynolds. William also has experience as a human resources manager in a Fortune 200 company, where he focused on integration of corporate culture and succession planning.

Prior to executive search, William led growth and innovation in churches in North Carolina, Alabama, and Houston.

During his time in Alabama, William had the chance to help rebuild and relocate an ailing congregation and lead them to new levels of growth. At age thirty-one he was elected Senior Pastor for the First Presbyterian Church of Houston, a church of about five thousand adults and fifteen hundred children. It is Houston's oldest congregation.

William is regularly invited to speak across the country in both church services and as a resource to churches and conferences on leadership and staffing. His book *Next: Pastoral Succession That Works,* on effective pastoral leadership and succession, was released through Baker Books in September 2014.

William is a regular contributor to Forbes.com on the topic of faith and the workplace. His articles on staffing and team trends are featured in *Outreach* magazine and on Fortune.com, FastCompany.com, and Inc.com.

William holds degrees from Wake Forest University and Princeton Theological Seminary.

Besides helping connect churches with key staff and preaching, William spends a whole lot of time with family and connecting with people. He is an avid social networker. Whether connecting with friends, candidates for searches he is conducting, or church members, he loves to network, and he would love to interact with you on social media @ wvanderbloemen.

He and his wife, Adrienne, live in Houston with their seven children and poodle, Moses.

ABOUT VANDERBLOEMEN SEARCH GROUP

Vanderbloemen Search Group is a pastor search firm that helps churches find their key staff. The firm provides customized, in-depth consulting services for executive search, succession planning, compensation analyses, and staff health.

What began with William Vanderbloemen on a card table in his home has grown to a team of more than thirty full-time Vanderbloemen team members called to help churches find the right people for their teams, combining the best practices of corporate executive search with years of pastoral experience.

Based in Houston, Texas, the Vanderbloemen Search Group team has helped hundreds of churches and faith-based organizations around the world with staffing and succession planning. Helping churches of all sizes in more than seventy-five different denominations/tribes, Vanderbloemen Search Group is uniquely geared to help churches through effective staff transitions.

Vanderbloemen Search Group has nine values that guide our team as we seek to serve God and our clients with excellence:

1. Broadband Love

We're a company built on the values of our Christian faith. As a company, we endeavor to live in grace and walk in love. We strive to show love to each client and candidate with whom we interact.

2. Unusual Servanthood

We exist to serve our clients and candidates in a way that makes them say, "I've never been treated like that by a company."

3. Wow-Making Excellence

We can't promise to be all things to all people, but we can strive to be all things to our clients. We endeavor to under-promise and over-deliver through each step of the search process. We also work to be a thought leader in the search industry, creating top-notch articles and resources to help organizations follow staffing and leadership best practices.

4. Ridiculous Responsiveness

In the world of smart phones, the world is at our fingertips. Quality comes first, but speed comes next. We want to deliver quality service at lightning speed.

5. Solution-Side Living

The Vanderbloemen team members are problem solvers, always having a solution mentality and not a victim mentality.

6. Ever-Increasing Agility

Being flexible is too rigid. We strive for agility to serve our clients and candidates with excellence in an ever-changing marketplace. Each employee at Vanderbloemen has "other duties as required" built into their job description.

7. Stewardship of Life

We measure success on our ability to maintain personal and corporate financial, spiritual, physical, and vocational boundaries. Each employee is required to give charitably of his or her time, talent, and resources.

8. Constant Improvement

Vanderbloemen Search Group strives for *kaizen*, the Japanese business philosophy of continuous improvement of working practices and personal efficiency. Each Vanderbloemen employee has an insatiable curiosity for making systems and processes better. The marketplace is changing daily, and Vanderbloemen Search Group strives to stay ahead of the curve by constantly asking, "How can we improve?"

9. Contagious Fun

We take our work seriously but not ourselves. Vanderbloemen loves what we do, and our joy for helping our clients is contagious. You'll often find us at a local restaurant enjoying each other's company after work hours, because we genuinely like each other.

Whether you're a church facing transition or a pastor considering your own future, we would be glad to visit with you and find out how we can help.

Contact the Vanderbloemen Search Group by e-mailing info@vanderbloemen.com or calling 713–300–9665.

ACKNOWLEDGMENTS

Any success I have with this book and our work at Vanderbloemen Search begins and ends with Jesus. I could never do what I do now, had He not ordered all of my scattered career steps that led up to now.

In a close second is my wife, Adrienne. She is the epitome of a steel magnolia, and her support, wisdom, and insight helped me launch, grow, and run our firm. I turn to her for counsel before all others and trust her discernment above anyone else I know.

Also key to the writing of this book is the team at Vanderbloemen Search Group. They are the finest group of people I have ever gotten to work with, and their contribution to this project has been essential to its completion and success.

Particular thanks go to a few team members who went the extra mile to help with the book. Holly Tate, Katie Viscontini, and Sarah Robins spent countless hours helping me with the material here and deserve major props. Bethany Brewster, who runs my life, was (as always) an enormous help. Thanks to all of you for making this happen.

Also to Devin Maddox of B&H, my editor who was the visionary for providing a search handbook for pastor search committees across the country. I'm grateful he asked us to provide this resource for the Church and for his wisdom along the way.

Through this group effort, I hope that this book becomes a lasting resource for the Church that helps congregations on the journey as they search for a new pastor.